LITERARY QUOTATION AND ALLUSION

LITERARY QUOTATION
AND ALLUSION

BY

E. E. KELLETT

KENNIKAT PRESS
Port Washington, N. Y./London

LITERARY QUOTATION AND ALLUSION

First published 1933
Reissued in 1969 by Kennikat Press
Library of Congress Catalog Card No: 70-86030
SBN 8046-0619-6

Manufactured by Taylor Publishing Company   Dallas, Texas

Contents

Chapter I

IF I open *Sartor Resartus*, and light on the sentence, "Thus Custom doth make dotards of us all," my mind is at once carried away to another place, and a little series of memories is started for me. The sentence has quite a different atmosphere, and quite a different force, from what it would have had if I had not known the original of which it is a kind of parody. And Carlyle *means* it to have this effect. If he had said "Custom makes us all fools," the substance of his remark would have been exactly the same; but it would have been comparatively empty.

Or again, when I read Macaulay on Halifax, whose "oratory is irretrievably lost to us, like that of many others who were accustomed to rise amid the breathless expectation of *senates*, and to sit down amidst reiterated bursts of *applause*"—when I read this, I know that, by the mere use of two particular words, Macaulay meant to call to his reader's mind the picture of a "country churchyard," with all its suggestions of shattered hopes and disappointed ambitions. The great are with the rude forefathers of the hamlet: the storied urn cannot call back the fleeting breath of the most persuasive of orators; and those who succeeded in commanding the applause of listening senates are now one with those whose "lot forbade": those who have gained renown are overtaken by the same oblivion which has overtaken the obscure. Alter "senates" to "assemblies" and "applause" to "cheers," and all these associations dissolve into nothingness : the charm is broken and they are escaped.

Some time ago I lit on the phrase, in a history of ancient times,[1] "Epicurus brought life—and *mortality* to light." One might almost say that this phrase, by means of its allusiveness, sums up the whole of Epicureanism : it is a very masterpiece of suggestive brevity. It tells us that the philosophy was a Gospel, that its founder set before him a healing aim, that he preached a religion and a rule of life—but with one thing lacking which Christianity supplied. If the reader will try to express the same thing in his own words, he will at once perceive the gain in terseness, vigour, and liveliness due to this simple half-quotation —so obvious when made that one feels one might have hit on it oneself, and yet an original and quite novel discovery.

Let me, at the risk of wearying the reader, give one more example.

A friend of mine, writing to me the other day about that stupendous mathematician, Ramanujan, who died too young, used the phrase, "Had he lived, we should have known something." How vastly does this sentence gain when we remember that these were the words used by Newton of Roger Cotes, whom also the Fates just showed to the world and then removed from sight !

A very interesting question arises as I ponder over these few instances of literary allusion, and the many others which turn up with almost every page I read—

[1] *Cambridge Ancient History*, Vol. VII, 233.

a question to which, as to most of the questions which really interest us, no answer can be given. Who first hit on the device of gaining force, or adding ornament, by stealing from someone who had gone before him? Let not familiarity blind us to the greatness of that man. Such allusiveness seems easy to us to-day : all of us have the seed, and can raise the flower without trouble. But he who first hit on it must indeed have been a genius : he was an original by virtue of his very scorn of originality. Here is a man who steals, and boasts of his thefts : he covers his walls with paintings, and openly proclaims they are taken from a National Gallery. He is not like the Spartan boy who stole and gained glory if undetected : he *desires* to be detected, and deliberately leaves clues to guide his pursuers to their prey. He says, "Here is a theft from Homer—track it down, and none will rejoice more than I when it is found." To have seen that he could give an added pleasure to his hearers by stirring their memories in this fashion, by making them recognise the old in the new, required insight of a high order.

Recollect also that, for the success of this device, we have to assume the existence of an audience capable of appreciating it. The first poet who, *with this intention*, borrowed from another, must have been aware that there were, among his hearers, at least some who would know enough to feel the little thrill he desired to give them ; for otherwise his poem would fail. Now thus to understand your public "craves a kind of wit." As, according to Viola, the court-fool must observe the quality of the persons on whom he jests—and this demands wisdom—so the man who quotes for effect must study those in whose ears he quotes : and it is clear then that, in addition to poetic talent, the first inventor of this device must have been a keen student of human nature. He must have watched his men, and carefully noted how much they could understand.

I imagine, however, that in reality he was not one but many. Like the inventor of the wheel, the steam-engine, or wireless telegraphy, he was not a man but a long succession of men, groping slowly and painfully towards the perfect machine, and his work may have taken centuries : the more so as the public to which he appealed had to be taught what he was doing. He may, very likely, have been regarded, in the first instance, as a common robber, and have suffered accordingly : nor, even now, are readers always able to distinguish between the true man and the thief who has made another's stolen apparel fit himself. We know that there were would-be critics, even in Virgil's time, so blind as not to see what the poet intended by this kind of borrowing. They told Virgil he had *stolen* from Homer. Virgil answered. "Steal in my fashion if you can. *You* will find it as easy to rob Hercules of his club as to rob Homer of a single line" : and even with the aid of a band of friends it took Virgil some time to explain the process to the general Roman public ; although he was by no means the first to annex Greek territory to Latin dominion. Much more, in all probability, was this the fate of a Virgil three or four thousand years before in an uncultivated society. That early poet, whether one man or a school, must have had a hard time, as all literary pioneers have hard times. He must have found that it was necessary to educate his public before they would listen to him in the right way : and he must have had patience as well as genius. If it took Wordsworth forty years to get Englishmen to read him, it may have taken this man a hundred as he laboriously explained, by example and precept, how there are some kinds of stealing that are laudable.

Or the practice may have arisen, and I think more probably, in a totally different manner. It may have begun merely with the prudent and economical use of materials provided by others. A man is not to blame if in rebuilding a cathedral which has been destroyed, he avails himself of the bricks and stones of the old structure : and early writers were in special need of such aids. It is hard for us to realise with what difficulty, at first, phrases were framed, and a vocabulary assembled, that might be adapted to any higher purpose than the mere necessities of daily converse. Men had words and phrases for their food, their drink, their hunting ; but when it came to recording events, describing battles, uttering exhortations, they were often at a loss. No dictionaries, no Roget's *Thesaurus*, were at their elbows. They had no collection, such as was once made for the Icelandic bards, of neatly alliterating "kennings"[1] which would run beautifully into their lines of verse. Even now, poets are said to tear their hair when a rhyme evades them : much more then. No wonder if they pounced with eagerness on

[1] Such as "the hair of Earth" for grass, or "the bone-gnat" for the sword.

words which some predecessor had used, and which
would save them the trouble of selecting words of
their own.   That even Homer did this is more than
likely : his poems bear all the marks of being centos,
and we do not need the authority of Kipling to induce
us to believe it.   One thing at any rate is not probable
but certain : Homer stole from *himself*.   When he had
once said something, and wished to say it again, he did
not pause to invent new collocations ; he used
exactly the old words.   And he had every excuse ;
for even so well equipped a writer as John Morley,
three thousand years later, with all the accumulations
of centuries at hand, did precisely the same thing.   In
writing on Burke comparatively late in life, he copied
out whole paragraphs of an essay he had written years
before.

Nor are we left to mere conjecture.   There is a well-
known and exquisite passage in Isaiah, on the Moun-
tain of the Lord.   The same passage occurs in Micah,
and very justifiably ; for, whoever was its original
author, it is pretty certain that even the sublime
genius of Isaiah,[1] even the high gifts of Micah, could
not have improved on it.   The borrower therefore,
Isaiah or Micah or both, took it without scruple.
Similarly, almost the whole prophecy of Obadiah is
found, practically verbatim, in the forty-ninth chapter
of Jeremiah.   Whether one borrowed from the other,
or both from an earlier seer, can never be known.
What is certain is that at least one of them, feeling that

---

[1] See also Isa. xvi. 13, where he tells us he is quoting an old prophecy : and compare Jer. xlviii.   The "Second Isaiah" (lii) quotes
from Nahum (i. 15).

the words said what he wanted to say, saw no reason why he should not use them. In those lucky days there was no copyright; literature was a common land on which you could graze your flocks at will : and authors stole words and sentences as calmly as Shakespeare stole his plots or Handel his themes. We thus find whole schools of writers using a style and a vocabulary so distinctive, and yet such a common possession, that we can mark off the schools from each other with absolute certainty, while remaining pretty sure that each school consisted of many writers. This is the case with that remarkable band of authors known to biblical critics by the symbol *P*. They probably cover several generations, yet their style is always the same, and always markedly different from that of the other Pentateuchal writers. Their vocabulary is so personal and characteristic that a single word is often enough to assure us that *P* is writing, and no one else. Having once got a style, they stuck to it, and never went outside it. But if they had occasion to quote from another school, quote they did, and left the ancient words unaltered.

Now let us imagine, as but one out of a hundred possible types, an early prose writer who has to touch on a subject already dealt with by a poet. Imagine, for instance, some primitive Herodotus having to narrate an incident of the Trojan War, or a Hebrew chronicler who has to tell of Sihon's victory over the Moabites. The one quotes a dozen lines of Homer, the other the nameless poet of "Woe unto thee, Moab, thou art undone, O people of Chemosh." This, in the first instance is purely a matter of business.

The thing has been said before ; why labour to give it a new dress ? There is, so far, no perception that the verse is better than the prose, or even essentially different from it : it is easy to remember, and that is nearly all about it. But let us imagine that our writer is a man of genius,[1] who at this moment has a flash of inspiration. Let us suppose that, having set down his quotation he surveys it and sees that the quotation is an *ornament*. It has, he perceives, lent force, beauty, or variety to his style. Set in the midst of his prose, it is like a jewel in its foil. By putting where it now is, *he*, the borrower, has become its second author : he has rights to it, and it is in a sense his own. Having seen the effect of chance, he conceives the idea of achieving the same, or a greater, effect by design. He is like the Phoenician sailors who have accidentally manufactured glass, and start to make their fortunes by repeating, of set purpose, the processes of nature. His writing, thenceforward, is variegated with verses from this poet or the other, with lines, half-lines, or single words from his well-stored memory. The discovery has been made : the example has been set, and other men follow.

Further discoveries, of course, remain to be made. It will not be long before our author learns, sometimes by painful experience, to apply the principle at which I hinted above, that he must know his audience. Unless that audience recognises his ornament for what

[1] Thus Snorri, in his *Heimskringla*, deliberately uses the verses of bards as *authorities :* they are to him what Luttrell's *Diary* or Pepys is to Macaulay. But I think he also feels that his history is enriched and adorned by his quotations ; that they add to the picturesqueness of his narrative, and that the reader will *enjoy* them.

it is, it will fail to adorn. Those whom he addresses
must at least perceive that the quotation *is* a quotation,
or his pride will suffer a sad fall : and often he finds
that he does not receive his full meed of praise unless
the quotation not only is known to be one, but is
actually a known and familiar one. He learns, as
orators learn, that the audience is in part the maker of
the speech, and the public largely the author of the
book. You must not go beyond your public. If you
allude, you must allude to what it knows. This is a
main law of Literary Reminiscence : do not, except
with due precautions, remind your readers of what
they do not remember.

Few rules, however, are oftener broken. A reviewer
of *Sartor Resartus* complained that the phrase "Bapho-
mctic Firebaptism" was beyond him ; and, though the
phrase certainly adds immensely to the force of the
passage in which it occurs, for those who understand
it, it is bewildering and annoying to those who, like
the reviewer, have never heard it before. Similarly,
many of Carlyle's mathematical allusions (he had
studied mathematics at the University) seem pedantic
to those who find the Four Rules sufficient. When he
compares the tangled diplomacy of Europe to "the
irreducible case of equations," it is certain that half his
readers will miss the point.[1] And if Carlyle, in the
nineteenth century of our era, made mistakes like this,
we may be sure that a writer of the tenth century B.C.
made many similar mistakes, till the painful experience
of which I spoke taught him the due limits of his art.
He would, however, learn more quickly than Carlyle :

[1] See note at the end of this chapter.

for an ancient author, whose public consisted of *hearers*, was in close contact with it than a modern author writing in his study and appealing to distant *readers*. When Herodotus recited to the Athenians, he could hardly fail to notice immediately what took and what fell flat.

A modern author, in fact, has to guess at the kind of public he is likely to gain, and his allusions may therefore often fail through no fault of his own. His very success may in this respect be against him. Macaulay, for instance, writing for the *Edinburgh Review*, could quote Greek, Latin, or Italian and be pretty sure his readers would understand. He could also indulge liberally in Biblical allusions. But his audience to-day is different. He is read by thousands who know no Greek, and to whom the Bible is almost a sealed book. Whole passages, therefore, seem tame which, when they were first written, were full of life.[1] Or the author's public may enlarge in space as well as in time. He may be read abroad : and then, though his more obvious merits may be visible, the atmosphere of his allusions will be lost. I remember very clearly showing a page of a very allusive author to a friend of mine, an Englishman who had been educated in Germany. The page contained no fewer than thirteen veiled quotations. My friend could speak English as well as I : but, his reading having been mainly in German literature, every one of the quotations passed him by ; as, doubtless, similar allusions in a German

---

[1] This I have proved by experience. I have read to certain audiences a dozen passages of Macaulay containing Scriptural allusions : and not one of the allusions has been recognised even *as* an allusion : much less has the context of the original been recalled.

author of the same kind would pass *me* by. He complained that there was no hint to give him warning : there ought, at least, he said, to have been inverted commas. But I objected that this would have drawn *too much* attention to the quotations : the author's desire was simply to give the reader a *slight* titillation of the memory—a gentle feeling that this was the old refurbished. "Every scribe" brings out of his treasury "things both new and old" ; but if he emphasises the antiquity, he spoils the novelty. Or, to parody another parable, if he deliberately *points out* that the new garment has an old patch, the rent is made too obvious. None the less, my friend's experience should teach an author that the allusions ought not to be beyond the range of the *majority* of his possible readers.

Again, I think it will be agreed that this particular author was somewhat too liberal of his allusions.[1] The page to which I refer was like a Russian icon, too heavily loaded with pearls. These ornaments should be used sparingly, or they cease to charm and finally cloy. The suspicion may arise in the mind of the reader that the writer cannot make a phrase of his own, but has to rely on his memory or on a commonplace-book to express the most ordinary idea : and, even if the quotations are all striking, few things weary more than a continual series of sparkles. A little dulness is by no means a bad feature in writing ; and helps to set off an occasional brilliancy : but neverending brilliancy has a habit of darkening with excess

[1] A censure which, I think, may be justly passed on that otherwise excellent writer, C. E. Montague.

of bright. We cannot read more than a few of La
Rochefoucauld's maxims at a sitting.

I shall illustrate these points somewhat more fully
later. These few hints may be sufficient for the
present : they show, at any rate, that the questions I
raised, though we cannot answer them, relate to
matters of considerable interest. We should indeed
like to know who first adorned a writing, a speech,
or a recitation, with a passage from another man's
work : what critic first blamed an allusion for being
too trite, too obscure, or too ostentatious : who first
drew, more or less exactly, the lines dividing quotation
from plagiarism. A device that gradually grew into
a recognised stylistic engine, until, as in the days of
Pitt and Fox, the House of Commons watched a piece
of oratory moving on from point to point, to culminate
in the *expected* passage from Virgil or Horace—a device
like this is well worth tracing from its beginnings to
its climacteric.

It would be pleasant, also, though it is usually quite
impossible, to know who first gives a *particular*
quotation its vogue. Such knowledge would throw
light equally on the quoted passage and on the
quoter. Who first, for instance, repeated in another
connection one of those verses of *Hamlet* which are
now so familiar that we use them without thinking of
their origin ? Who first applied to new uses one of
Marlowe's mighty lines ? Such a man must, unconsciously, have felt that those lines had a universal
appeal : he must have had something of the gift of
the man who makes a proverb : nor is there much less
genius in setting the words of others in an unexpected

context than in inventing striking phrases of one's own. There is, it is true, much chance in it. I have known reviewers of a poem, who, admiring some stanza of the poet's, have set it in the forefront of their criticism, plainly hoping thus to make it popular : and they have failed. In especial, I recall a reviewer so doing with a work of William Watson—a writer who, whatever his limitations, is assuredly a master of the single sounding line. But the verse thus quoted has remained unfamiliar to the general. The unknown man who set "Thereby hangs a tale" running round the world was more in sympathy with the common mind than this learned critic : and, if he knew what he was doing, must have smiled as he noticed people thinking they were quoting Shakespeare who were really quoting *him*. Such quotations become part and parcel of our speech, and go on till, like "One touch of nature makes the whole world kin," they say what Shakespeare never meant, or, like "fresh fields and pastures new," say what Milton never said.

I confess also that I should, in certain moods, like to know who first neatly and dexterously *capped* a quotation : who, seeing that it had had its effect on an audience, by a skilful twist deprived it of its force in one direction and turned it to his own advantage. In the debate on the Reform Bill, Gladstone and Lowe thus alternately capped each other's references to the Trojan Horse : it would be a pleasure to learn what two orators first "scored points" over each other in this particular manner. We shall never know, but we cannot help wondering ; and the wonder may perhaps incite us to conjectures not altogether vain.

"What song the Sirens sang"—but I must not, after censuring triteness, myself indulge in the tritest of allusions.

There are certain distinctions, perhaps obvious, which it may yet be advisable to mark at the outset of our little inquiry. In one sense *all*, or practically all, our writing is quotation. A thousand years of writing have given us a set of vocabularies, each appropriated to particular uses : and no man can write without employing multitudes of phrases the associations of which have been fixed long since and cannot be *deliberately* altered. This dialect for poetry, that for history, the other for philosophy, yet another for business : the plain style, the ornate style, the conversational, the elaborate : our variations on whichever of these styles we choose must range within pretty narrow limits. But our use of these styles and of the chosen phraseology is neither allusion nor quotation.

Again, I am not about to speak of quotation which is used for any other end than the adornment or heightening of our own style. An historian who gives a passage from a previous writer in order to correct it, a critic who copies twenty lines of a poem in order to appraise it—neither of these comes within my purview. Nor, except in special cases, does an author who excerpts a lengthy passage by way of *illustrating* his own remarks. The quotations and allusions on which I propose to dwell are those which cannot, without violence, be detached from their context ; they are woven into the piece, and are part and parcel of the writer's work. He has, at least in intention, made them his own ; and the degree of success

with which he has carried out that intention is what
I wish to judge.

For instance—since a concrete example may be
clearer than any number of generalities—I shall pay no
attention to such quotations as those with which
Dr. Samuel Smiles diversifies *Self-Help* or *Character*.
These were done with scissors and paste, and, so far
from improving the texture of Smiles's work, make
it an abomination of tessellation.   On the other hand,
take Tennyson's

> This way and that dividing the swift mind
> In act to throw.

This is a theft from Virgil.   My business will be to
inquire whether it is too pedantic, or whether, in the
minds of the right readers, it does not start a series of
undulating suggestions which altogether transform it
from a mere set of words into what, almost without
exaggeration, may be called an apocalyptic vision.
Tennyson *meant* his readers to see whence it came and
whither it pointed ; has he succeeded or has he failed ?
The literary alluder walks along a steep and narrow
road : on one side is pedantry or obscurity, and he
may often be justly charged with ostentation, with
quoting vaingloriously or for quoting's sake.   I have
known a clergyman who regaled a village congregation with extracts from Descartes.   On the other
hand looms the pit of triteness or insipidity : the man
may be quoting what everybody knows too well or
what is not worth repeating.   I have heard orators
make a great parade of erudition by citing the names
of great men who happen to have said that life is a
battle or that teachers need patience.   I shall, as I

proceed, try to show how far such orators have kept their feet on this difficult and delusive pass.

In one word, I am dealing here with allusions that are, either actually or in intent, artistic. I am sorry to have to use that word ; for there is none for which I harbour a more utter detestation. It has the proud distinction of being associated with more humbug than any other, even "psychology" or "complex" being a poor second. The cant talked in the name of art is sometimes nothing less than nauseous, and reminds one of the tyrannical crimes committed in the name of Liberty. But unfortunately there are occasions when the word has to be used : there is no other that serves my purpose. I promise the reader, however, that he shall be afflicted with it, in this little book, as rarely as possible.

———

Note.—A remarkable instance of failure in appreciation due to missing an allusion is provided by no less a critic than Longinus. He says that Plato is ridiculed for speaking in a certain fashion about gold and silver wealth. Now Verrall shows that here Plato is clearly quoting from a play : and when this is recognised, the passage ceases at once to be flat, and becomes vivid and pointed. Elsewhere Longinus censures Xenophon and Timaeus for "frigidity," whereas, as Verrall again points out, both are quoting, and the frigidity is at once seen to be imaginary.

Chapter II

MUCH of the pleasure derived by the reader from a quotation or allusion is that of recognition—one of the earliest pleasures of which the human mind is susceptible. We can observe this in the behaviour of children when they see some person or thing they have seen before, and at once give it a name. In their case the recognition is often very inexact; they will greet a dog as "pussy" or any man as "daddy." With the advance of knowledge we become more precise; a bird is no longer a bird merely, but a black-cap or a yellow-hammer; a tree no longer a tree but a maple or an ash. The pleasure of recognition, however, is always there, and in a healthy mind it remains keen. In literature the same thing is visible; we are pleased when we detect an identity. This was noticed long ago by Aristotle. "When we see things reproduced with exact fidelity," says he in the *Poetics*, "we view them with delight. To discover in this fashion gives lively pleasure, not merely to philosophers, but to men in general. For instance, when men see a likeness, they enjoy it because they can say 'That is he'; whereas, if you happen not to have seen the original, your pleasure has to be gained not from contemplating the imitation as such, but from noting how skilfully the picture is wrought, or coloured, or the like."

Now this kind of pleasure, as Aristotle points out, is more easily felt by the ordinary man than that given by skill in execution, which can, in its fulness, be perceived only by the expert. A melody that is well-known is almost always immediately enjoyed by the multitude : a strange one takes time, and only the musician can at once appreciate its technical merits. A writer using a quotation is in the position of the portrait-painter or of the singer of a familiar air. He can be tolerably sure of arousing the pleasure of recognition in his readers—provided, of course, the quotation *is* recognised. *Every* reader, on seeing the passage, feels a slight enjoyable titillation ; whereas it takes a stylist, or at least one who has studied style, to appreciate the subtler play of the author's diction. Anyone who will go back to his own beginnings in reading will recall that among the passages he most enjoyed were those containing a quotation he, even so early, could detect and assign to its origin. I myself well remember how, at thirteen or fourteen, I thus noted certain quotations in Farrar's ill-fated *Eric*, and how the book, on that account, was read with a zest it might otherwise not have earned. Conversely, when one has read a quotation without knowing where it comes from, the discovery of its first home gives a thrill. Thus, after reading in *St. Winifred's* "Nemo repente fuit turpissimus," or "Virtutem videant intabescantque relicta," it was, as I clearly recollect, a positive delight to hit upon the original passages, months or years later, in Juvenal or Persius. There may, it is true, be a little vanity mingled with this pleasure ; the reader may, overtly or subconsciously, be pluming himself on his knowledge and detective acumen.   But that is all to the advantage of the *author* ; it helps to create a sympathy between him and the reader, and begets a liking which carries the reader through many subsequent pages.   It is a gentle kind of flattery ; and we all like to be flattered. "You," the writer says in effect, "are a person of culture, and while I should not venture to set such a puzzle to others, I am sure *you* will be able to solve it."

When a Parliamentary orator, as once happened, referred in his speech to Oropesa, to Squillaci, to the commerce of the Caesars, and brought the House down, this was because he was paying a compliment to their intelligence.   Not one in twenty had ever heard of Oropesa or Squillaci ; but they liked to fancy that they were supposed to have all this history at their fingers' ends, and cheered their flatterer to the echo.   For a similar reason, some very learned preachers attract large audiences, who are pleased to imagine themselves to belong to the select band that can appreciate them.   When the preacher quotes Kant or Hegel they nod happily ; it is not everybody who could understand that !   Much of the popularity of Browning in England, or of Hebbel in Germany, when once a hearing had been gained, was due to this cause, which explains also that "appeal to the best class of our readers" made by the editor of the *Edinburgh Review*, when he wished to induce them to stomach Macaulay's hundred-page essay on Bacon ; the sort of appeal which, as Macaulay's biographer says, never fails of success.   I think it will not seldom be found that the popularity of "best-sellers" is, at least in part, attained by this means. A few dexterous allusions, just within the compass of the ordinary reader, set in motion the sympathetic feelings of which I have spoken, and enlist the reader's harmless *amour-propre* on the author's side. When once the *rapport* has been established, a friendly attention is secured. Some authors, I suspect, are shrewd enough to throw in a few of their allusions for the benefit of the critics, and thus earn a favourable review.

Even experts, or, as Aristotle calls them, "philosophers," are subject to these influences, and perhaps the more so in some cases because they think themselves superior to them. They recognise the allusions more speedily than the commonalty, and pass them over more lightly. They may often regard them as trivial ; but below the surface of their minds they feel them. Though the higher virtues of a style are more visible to them than to others, they cannot quite escape the force of the lower ; and the detection of a veiled quotation, which the ordinary man misses altogether, cannot but cause them a certain exhilaration. If, to take a crude example, the author uses the word "anfractuosity," an expert, seeing the reference to Dr. Johnson, experiences just that satisfaction which the common man experiences when he detects the coarser and more obvious borrowings. He likes to feel himself a polite Granville or a knowing Walsh : and he is, at this very moment, glowing with mild elation as his mind rapidly traces to its source the allusion I have just made, and realises that it is caviare to the general.

It goes without saying—though I said it in the preceding chapter—that the author must bear his chosen audience always in his mind ; and suit his allusions, as he suits everything else, to their comprehension. If he is writing for a large and miscellaneous public, he must remember the prejudice against the "highbrow." Exactly as the common man is pleased with an allusion which he recognises, so he is annoyed with one that is beyond him. It demands skill to make an obscure allusion tell—to get it, in the American phrase, "across the footlights." There are occasions when we have to prepare our readers for what is coming, and to explain, as delicately as possible, our quotation ; but delicacy is indeed necessary. We have to feel our way, and perhaps to make as many turns and twists as Polonius recommended to Reynaldo for manipulating Laertes. Above all, we must abstain from all appearance of pedagogy. The common reader dislikes the schoolmaster, and resents any obtrusive piece of instruction. We have therefore to steer, as cleverly as may be, between Scylla and Charybdis. Carlyle's unprepared allusion to "Baphometic fire-baptism" irritated the reviewer ; but if he had devoted half a page to describing the ceremony, other reviewers, or even the same one, might have been equally fretted ; the more so as it is a human weakness to imagine that what we have only just learned we have known all our lives. On the other hand, we feel a just resentment when we are blamed for not recognising that Mr. E. E. Cummings's poem "Sunset" is based on Rémy de Gourmont's *Litanies de la Rose*, or that its thirty-one words are a reminiscence of the dominant

c

Japanese verse-form.   Mr. Cummings might at least have given us a hint.[1]

But, while we have a right to demand that a reference to Rémy de Gourmont should be made clear, there is an opposite danger.   The quotation must not be too familiar : and here once more the word "too" turns out to be ambiguous and question-begging.   What is too much for one man may be insufficient for another. I said above that concert-goers like to hear what they have heard before.   But if they have heard it too often, they will not like it at all.   Who, however, can tell what "too often" means for each and all of the audience ?   Triteness is at least as relative as up and down.   Here there is nothing for it but that the author should exercise his tact as well as he can, and at any rate, beware of increasing the triteness of a

---

[1] This poem runs thus :

SUNSET

"Stinging
gold swarms
upon the spires
silver

chants the litanies the
great bells are ringing with rose
the lewd fat bells
        and a tall

wind is dragging
the sea
        with
dream

—S

An explanation of it, whether ironical or otherwise is hard to say, is given by Miss Laura Riding and Mr. Robert Graves, who tell us, truly enough, that "it is written with no feelings of obligation to the plain reader."

verse or a well-known maxim by quoting it himself "too often." Let not his readers be tempted to complain that he has but a small store of quotations, and recurs to the same source *ad nauseam*. As a man "noscitur a sociis," so some writers are known by their favourite tags, and are disliked accordingly. Even if the tag is the author's own, he should be sparing in the use of it. Matthew Arnold's "sweetness and light" was borrowed, but he used it till it cloyed. Carlyle's "Sea-green Incorruptible" was to all intents and purposes original; but it has wearied more people than it has amused; and Scott's "Glorious John," though remembered, is not remembered with gratitude.

The quotation must further be felt to be apt, to fit neatly into its place, to clinch what has just been said, and to be more brief, more pointed, or otherwise more telling, than words in the author's ordinary style would have been.[1] If, for instance, it be from a foreign language, it must justify its migration; it must be, in its present place, more effective than anything English could be. How many French quotations, which crowd the pages of certain writers, might better have been left where they were! Though given in the most impressive of italics, they are too

[1] Lord Acton's hundred and five quotations illustrating the twenty-eight pages of his Inaugural Lecture are a staring case in point. Acton's learning was so stupendous that he could never say anything without recalling where and when it had been said before: and as a result, he loads his pages with passages, often quite ordinary in style and expression, from authors in half-a-dozen languages. Again and again these passages, collected laboriously in the appendix, turn out to be weaker than the sentence of Acton's own which they are meant to strengthen. But, as they *are* in an appendix, they do not weaken the actual lecture.

often perceived to be but ordinary and feeble *clichés*, all the more intolerable for being pretentious. They are as needless as the alexandrine which moved the contempt of Pope.

Again, they must stop at the right point. By this I do not merely mean that they must not be too long. They must stop where their appropriateness ceases. Denman's fatal continuation of "Neither do I condemn thee" to "go and sin no more," ruined the whole of his otherwise convincing demonstration that Queen Caroline had not sinned at all. A Yorkshire local preacher, observing that there were twelve at a prayer-meeting, remarked that that was just the number of the Apostles, but unluckily added, "And one of them was a devil." Equally unfortunate is it if the context of the quotation, being inappropriate, is so familiar that it irresistibly occurs to the hearer, and provides an obvious retort. Palmerston's words to the Sabbatarian Wilberforce, who would not drive to Church, "How blest is he who ne'er consents by ill-advice to walk," presented the Bishop with a simple and gratuitous repartee.[1]

After the disaster of 1886, when Gladstone's Home-Rule Bill was defeated, he met his supporters, and bade them consult

> How to overcome this dire calamity,
> What reinforcement they might gain from hope,
> If not, what resolution from despair.

The Tories were not slow to point out that these were the words of Satan, the only being they were, at that time, willing to allow to be more demoniac than

[1] Nor stands in sinners' ways, nor sits where men profanely talk.

Gladstone.   Quotations are often two-edged weapons, and have to be handled with care.

Much of what I have been saying may be specially illustrated by a reference to verbal parody, which is obviously only a particular species of quotation. Such parody will, as a rule, lose much of its effect if the original is unfamiliar. Should we be ignorant of the line "Here the first roses of the year shall blow," Catherine Fanshawe's substitution of "noses" for "roses" will leave us unmoved. "Sweet are the uses of advertisement" is flat and feeble unless it leads us to the Forest of Arden ; and "the short and simple flannels of the poor" must, to gain even its tiny modicum of applause, transport us from the village cricket-pitch to the elegiac country churchyard. But also the parody must have a worth and meaning of its own ; and the metamorphosed quotations must be forceful and pointed in their new setting. Precisely as the ordinary quotation or allusion must make us feel it has, for the time being, gained by being transplanted, so the parody must be felt to have thrown a new light upon its original, and revealed capacities in it which we did not suspect. It must be a sort of corollary to the original, deducing from the theorem conclusions latent in it all the while, but not perceived till the geometer has drawn them out. "We are seven," which has been so often parodied, has, I think, been enlarged in range by many of its parodists, and made to signify more than it did before.

Yet again, the parody, like the direct quotation, must be unforced : there must be no sign of hard labour or of long research about it. The ideal parody

must read like an original, and give the idea that it
sprang up naturally in the author's mind. It follows a
model, but it must follow it *passibus aequis*. Even
when it startles by its ingenuity, we must be betrayed
into the belief that the ingenious twist came unbidden.
If we suspect that Pope has looked up his Virgil or
his Homer, of set purpose, in order to variegate the
Rape of the Lock with burlesques, we are disillusioned,
and like the poem less. Still more do we despise an
author if we suspect that the striking phrase which
clinches his paragraph has come, not from the fulness
and readiness of his own mind, but from a handy
Dictionary of Quotations. If our parodist has over-
elaborated his jest, we cease to care for him. This is
why so many parodies which have begun pleasingly
because they sprang spontaneously from the author's
brain, receive no "praise in departing." He has set
himself doggedly to finish them, despite the recalcit-
rance of his Pegasus—and we see the strain.

A still better illustration of my point will be found
in what I may call an "anti-parody"—an attempt not
to degrade the original but to elevate it. Of this many
examples could be adduced from all sorts of places.
It is said that a beautiful chorale of Bach's was once
a vulgar tavern-air; and the theme of Chopin's
Funeral March has been heard crooned by the peas-
antry in the East of Europe. Bach and Chopin have
taken these themes and transmuted their brass to gold.
In scores of cases, Burns's most exquisite songs are
merely old Scottish folk-lays, often Rabelaisian,
similarly refined in the furnace of genius. Campbell's
Mariners of England did the same—except that less

refining was necessary—for *Ye Gentlemen of England ;*[1]
and in a sense Julia Ward Howe's "Mine eyes have
seen the coming of the glory of the Lord" is an "anti-
parody" of *John Brown's Body ;* it was, at any rate, a
deliberate attempt to drive out a somewhat empty
song by a solemn and inspiriting one.   But the most
remarkable of all these sublimators that I know is
Charles Wesley, who, on the principle that the devil
should have neither the best tunes nor the best words,
robbed secular poets, right and left, and turned their
words to the service of what he held to be religious
truth.   Out of a host of proofs I could adduce, I will
content myself with two or three.   Wesley found in
Prior—not a very pious poet—the line

' Love, like Death, makes all distinction void ';
and he turned the ordinary human love into the
ecstatic devotion of the saint :

> Love, like Death, hath all destroyed,
> Rendered all distinctions void :
> Names, and sects, and parties fall,
> Thou, O Christ, art all in all.

He took from an opera of Dryden's—a work worth
remembering solely because Purcell set it to music—
the song,

> Fairest isle, all isles excelling,
>   Seat of pleasures and of loves,
> Venus here shall choose her dwelling,
>   And forsake her Cyprian groves.

and made of it the famous hymn "Love divine, all
loves excelling."   Nay, he seized a lyric of Rochester's,

---

[1] We shall see later a very noteworthy instance of a like transmuta-
tion contrived by the magic of Virgil.

which it would be a euphemism to call light, and made of it something not far short of a psalm. As old Fuller might have expressed it, he compelled Helicon to flow into Jordan.

If then, as was very wisely observed long ago, a poet's readers miss much by not knowing what he has blotted,[1] it is plain that alike in parodies and in anti-parodies we shall miss much if we do not know the originals. We must have the chance of seeing how skilfully, in the one case, the original has been turned to ridicule, and how nobly, in the other, it has been subdued to higher uses. We cannot admire Burns or Wesley as they should be admired unless we know the shapeless mass out of which they have hewn their statues. Recognition is thus, as I observed, a main element in our pleasure. But there is also more. The imitator must be perceived to be no slave, and mimicry must be felt to be also creation. It is as certain a mark of superhuman power to be able to metamorphose as to call from nothing into being. It takes Poseidon to create a horse : but it also takes Poseidon to turn a ship into a reef. To make a poem is a task of genius ; but even to make a parody of the poem, if the parody is good, shows, in its own sphere, genius too.

As a rule, then, it is tolerably clear that the best allusions will be those which lie beneath the surface : those that do not give the reader the sense that his author is always quoting, or that he depends upon others, but which whisper to him, almost inaudibly,

---

[1] A truth which Pope and Gray knew well. We *have* the chance, often, of noting their blots.

that the allusions are the natural overflow of a rich and
well-stored mind—like those echoes of Lucretius in
Virgil which show that the younger poet knew the
elder so well that he had forgotten how well he knew
him.   The reader should rise from a book with the
conviction, gained he hardly knows how, that this
writer is a reader too, and one who, selecting from the
books he has read their best things, has laid them
aside for use at the right time.   Nor is he only a
reader, with the fulness that choice and industrious
reading gives.   He has in addition the exactness
which Bacon ascribes to the good writer.   He does
not annoy the good reader by careless misquotation.
I have spoken above of Farrar, and of the pleasure
which his quotations gave me in my youth.   That
pleasure has been much diminished in later years, as
I have noticed that half of his quotations are inexact :
that, for instance, he gives Shelley's "tramples it to
fragments" as "shivers it to atoms," and treats other
poets with similar lack of respect.   In a lesser degree,
I think, a much greater writer also offends : Hazlitt's
numerous quotations from Shakespeare and Milton
were certainly not always verified.   Byron was right
in telling Campbell he ought to quote accurately ; he
did not invariably obey his own rule.

But Bacon speaks also of the conversationalist as a
"ready man" : and this too the good writer is ; he
unites the three virtues of exactness, abundance, and
quickness.   His allusions are *there ;* they start to his
mind when they are needed.   Like an accomplished
talker, he finds his good things immediately ; they
do not strike him the day after.   Or if, like Addison,

he has to draw on the bank for his money, he yet contrives to conceal his momentary poverty, and works his allusions in so skilfully that we never guess that his pockets have not all the while been jingling with small cash.

To sum up, in words that have often been used before, the true quoter is he whose thefts have become his own property, and who is so affluent that he has forgotten alike how much he has and where it came from.

Chapter III

It is well-known that Tennyson was charged by many, and specially by Churton Collins, with a somewhat exaggerated tendency to borrowing from earlier authors. Collins, whose verbal memory was prodigious, and whose capacity for seeing likenesses in difference was still greater, made a collection of Tennyson's imitations and reminiscences which filled a whole volume. The poet was sensitive to these charges, and angry with those who brought them.[1] He could not bear to be told that one of the most familiar of his stanzas had been anticipated by Lord Houghton.[2]

As *In Memoriam* has probably, in proportion, more of these borrowings than others of Tennyson's works, Andrew Bradley, in his edition of that poem, discusses the point. "It is essential," he says, "to distinguish the possible causes of the similarities of phrase here in question. Sometimes the poet adopts the phrase of an earlier writer knowingly, and with the intention that the reader should recognise it; and if the reader

[1] He was also vexed when his own verses were put to base employ. He could not forgive Sir William Harcourt for murmuring "The earliest pipe of half-awakened bards" in allusion to the poet's habit of smoking before breakfast.

[2] He who for love hath undergone
The worst that can befall,
Is happier thousandfold than one
Who never loved at all.

Cp. *In Mem.* xxvii. Houghton dates his poem 1830, three years before Hallam's death.

fails to recognise it he does not fully appreciate the passage. Milton and Gray often did this, and Tennyson does it to beautiful effect when he reproduces phrases of Virgil or Theocritus : and so *In Memoriam*, when he writes 'change their sky' or 'brute earth'[1] he means the Horatian phrases to be recognised."

Sometimes, adds Bradley, the similarity is due to mere coincidence ; sometimes again to unconscious reproduction,[2] a phrase is retained in the memory and comes out as if it were original. Thus, in another sphere, Sullivan once played over a beautiful air, and fancied it was his own, until a friend pointed out it was Beethoven's. It is probable that nearly every writer could provide something similar from his own experience.

I am inclined to think that most of Shakespeare's verbal borrowings, especially from Marlowe,[3] are of this unconscious kind. He could quote openly and at length from his great predecessor : "Shallow rivers to whose falls melodious birds sing madrigals," or

---

[1] Caelum, non animum, mutant qui trans marc currunt ; Ep. I, 11. Quo bruta tellus et vaga flumina, Odes, I, 34.

[2] Such, for instance, is undoubtedly Macaulay's famous "New Zealander" passage (Essay on Ranke's *History of the Popes*) ; "The Church of Rome may still exist in undiminished vigour when some traveller from New Zealand shall take his stand on a broken arch of London Bridge to sketch the ruins of St. Paul's !" a passage which occurs almost word for word in Mrs. Barbauld's poem entitled "1811." Macaulay must have read the poem in his childhood, and have retained it in his mind (substituting however, *London* Bridge for Blackfriars) till he thought it his own.
In another place, Macaulay confesses to an unconscious plagiarism from Johnson's *Rambler*. In a youthful essay the New Zealander appears in embryo.

[3] And from the old plays which he revised. I have noted a score of unconscious echoes from *Leir* and the *Famous Victories* : doubtless there are scores of others.

"Who ever loved, that loved not at first sight ? "   On
the other hand, he could make an allusion, knowing
that everyone would recognise it :

> Why, she is a pearl
> Whose price hath launched above a thousand ships.

But in other cases he was remembering without
knowing he was doing so. When writing the
Merchant of Venice his mind was steeped in the *Jew of
Malta*, as, later, it was in Plutarch.[1]   He may have
read it, or seen it, just before, and lines from it came
unbidden. "He that denies to pay shall straight become a Christian" : "Sawst thou not mine argosy at
Alexandria ?"   "O Abigail, that I had thee here too ;
O girl, O gold, O beauty, O my bliss !"   "I'll be thy
Jason, thou my golden fleece" : these are but a few
passages, recollections of which in the *Merchant* the
reader will at once recall ; and "I drank of poppy and
cold mandrake juice," "the heavens are just," "the
juice of hebon," not to mention others, are phrases
that stuck in Shakespeare's brain, to be reproduced in
later plays.

"Lastly, a poet may use the words of a predecessor,
knowing what he is doing but not intending the origin
of the phrase to be observed."   This is plagiarism.

I am going to speak briefly here of the first of these
four classes.   There have been whole schools of poets
who have made this a regular practice, and who may
almost be said to base on it their chief claim to repute.

---

[1] That Milton, like Shakespeare, knew the *Jew of Malta* intimately,
could be easily proved : compare "Ripping the bowels of the earth"
for money with "Rifling the bowels of their mother earth for treasures."

Such a poet is Horace in his *Odes*, who plainly wished his readers to see how beautifully he had dovetailed his borrowings into the texture of a lyric : how his words were so Latin that they might seem to be original, and fell into their context so naturally that their new abode seemed their birthplace ; while yet his instructed audience went back, inevitably, to Alcaeus or Sappho. In another fashion Virgil, aspiring to be to Rome what Homer was to Greece, borrowed not only lines and phrases, but the whole scheme of his epic from the Greek. Similarly, he openly avowed that his Eclogues were inspired by the "Sicilian Muse" : and half the beauty of whole passages lies in our remembering Sicily while we are in Lombardy. But more than this. He was to be the *national* poet of Rome, and therefore he took, without scruple, lines and phrases from previous poets like Ennius and Catullus.[1] See, he seemed to proclaim, I am the King of Latin song, and levy tribute on my subjects as a matter of right. He might have been saying, "cedite, Romani scriptores, cedite Grai," and as they retreated, he spoiled their camp.

Among English poets, as Bradley says, and as I have already pointed out on an earlier page, three stand, in this respect, pre-eminent. Milton pillages from Virgil as Virgil had pillaged from Homer and Theocritus ; but he also lays the whole of classical and Scriptural literature under contribution, and often

[1] Sometimes the result is what I have called an "anti-parody"—a sublimation of the original : as when he adapts the line about Berenice's hair—"Invita, O regina, tuo de *vertice* cessi"—and makes Aeneas use it to Dido in the shades : "Invitus, regina, tuo de *litore* cessi."

has two or three reminiscences in a single line.[1]   But
he also takes from English writers, knowing well that
they cannot complain.   To be quoted by Milton is
like being mentioned by Gibbon—it is to have your
name written on the dome of St. Paul's.[2]   Whether
"Which way I fly is hell, myself am hell" is a conscious
or unconscious borrowing from Marlowe may be
doubted, but the line is Milton's own, with the added
magic that it carries us in an instant all the way from
the "Archangel ruined" to the degraded and lost
Mephistophilis, the Machiavellian devil of *Dr. Faustus*.
And so the very first line of *Paradise Lost*, with its
proud reminiscence of Donne's

> That tree
> Whose fruit threw death on else immortal us,[3]

transfers our thoughts, for the moment, to an entirely
different world.   When Christ, in *Paradise Regained*,
borrows from Ben Jonson his words of contempt for
the "miscellaneous rabble"

> Of whom to be dispraised were no
> small praise,[4]

we think of the one extraordinary similarity between
two men otherwise the poles apart.   Jonson and
Milton were both profound and haughty scholars,

[1] Thus "mirth which after no repenting draws" refers us to Plato's
Timaeus, 59 : "pleasure that brings no repentance" ; as shown by
the fact that Plato has just been speaking of geometry ("Let Euclid
rest and Archimedes pause").   But Milton also has his eye no
Martial, x. 48 : "Accedunt sine felle ioci nec mane timenda Libertas."

[2] This is *not* an unconscious plagiarism from Thackeray, but a
deliberate theft.

[3] Divine Sonnets, ix.

[4] Ben Jonson's lines are :
> "If they spake worse, 'twere better, for of such
> To be dispraised is the most perfect praise."

aloof and lonely, caring for a fit audience even if few, and only too scornful of the "herd confused." Milton, desirous of expressing his scorn, borrows from the Poet-laureate of the Stuarts, and speaks with the same accent as that which Jonson used when his plays failed to please the mob. Milton would not despise the stage when Jonson's learned sock was on.[1] The stern phrases put on a peculiar impressiveness when we learn from whence they are drawn.

As for Gray, "the most learned man in Europe," who does not know that ever since Mitford, or earlier still, literary detectives have been searching out the sources of his tiny poetic output, and though they have found hundreds, have not yet discovered all ? Gray was primarily a student, and is pre-eminently the poet of students. The *Bard*, and the *Progress of Poesy*,[2] yield their treasures only to those who know. Even the *Elegy*, most English of poems, and making its appeal to the most universal of emotions, is a mosaic of allusions, and the more one learns, the more allusions one detects. Gray himself warns us that it is so : for a note to the very first line informs us that it is borrowed from Dante's "squilla di lontano," and bids us be on the lookout for other reminiscences

[1] Jonson himself was one of the most consummate and unblushing borrowers in our literature. Not only did he take whole scenes verbatim from Plautus, and whole speeches from Cicero or Tacitus, but his "Drink to me only with thine eyes," a patchwork from Philostratus, seems to me without exception the most exquisite "conveyance" in the English language : and the more so as no one would suspect it to be conveyed at all. Every word is borrowed, and every word is Jonson's own.

[2] A simple example is the two-word phrase "feathered king," in the *Progress*, which we are meant to refer to the *Phoenix and the Turtle* of Shakespeare. Even this loses if we do not so refer it.

throughout the poem. Nor are we disappointed :
here is a reminiscence of Lucretius, there one of
Horace, here a fragment from *As You Like It*, there a
phrase from Milton. Apollonius of Rhodes, Chaucer,
Virgil, Pope, Petrarch, Dryden, all and each contribute
their toll ; and yet who can deny that the poem is
Gray's all over—so much so that it is read with
delight by thousands who never suspect that it is of
composite authorship ? This is what allusiveness
should be : the transferred phrase should be felt to
be exactly right in its new place, while at the same
time it is full of memories of the old. It must be like
the skylark of Wordsworth's poem—true to the
kindred points of both its homes.

As with Gray, so with Tennyson. No poet in our
language is more capable of making phrases of his
own : none more marvellous in the skill with which
he annexes phrases from others. Bradley has chosen
for us one or two examples already : I will content
myself with but one more. In the early poem,
Eleanore, there is the passage—

> My heart a charmed slumber keeps
>   While I muse upon thy face ;
> And a languid fire creeps
>   Thro' my veins to all my frame,
> Dissolvingly and slowly ; soon
>   From thy rose-red lips MY name
> Floweth, and then, as in a swoon,
>   With dimming sound my ears are rife,
>   My tremulous tongue faltereth,
>   I lose my colour, I lose my breath,
>   I drink the cup of a costly death,
> Brimm'd with delicious draughts of
>   warmest life.

D

I was struck with the intensity of these lines in early youth, long before I knew they came from Sappho. But when I saw the original Greek, they acquired a new force and meaning : they came to me charged with all the passion of the Lesbian airs, with thoughts of a love so mighty that it yet lives after twenty-five centuries : a love translated into words so direct that every lover feels they speak for him, and will speak eternally. But this is not all. I remember that they were chosen by Catullus to speak *his* ill-fated love ; and they gain the added charm of memories of the poet and the woman he named the Lesbian : a love eternal like Sappho's, but ending in catastrophe and disillusion ;

Odi et amo : quare id faciam fortasse requiris :
Nescio ; sed fieri sentio et excrucior.

All this Tennyson felt, and meant his fit audience to feel.

There are other great poets whom Bradley might have mentioned. He might have referred to Spenser, who not only drew largely on Ariosto in the endeavour to "overgo" him, but translated, as literally as his stanza would permit, a "lovely lay" from Tasso : and indeed borrowed from everywhere in Virgilian style. He felt himself to be to Elizabeth what Virgil was to Augustus, and acted on that principle. More relevant still to our theme is Spenser's model, Chaucer. The number of quotations and allusions, long and short, direct and indirect, exact or loose, to earlier writers, in Chaucer's works is positively astounding, and every year of study adds more to the known amount.[1] Virgil, Ovid, Boethius, the Romance of the Rose, the Divine Comedy, the early Fathers, contemporary

[1] We shall know many more when Mr. Lowes's work appears.

preachers, Popes and pagans, he uses all, and uses them openly. As often as not, perhaps, he either names his victim or gives plain hints that he is quoting. In the margin of one manuscript are references, almost certainly by Chaucer himself, to his originals. But what I wish to emphasise is the fact that in practically every case the borrowed passage is exactly suited to its context, and that in many cases Chaucer's imitations are vast improvements on the things imitated. He is a copyist who betters what he copies. Let anyone compare, for instance, the passages which Chaucer takes from Statius with what they were before he took them, and then say candidly what he thinks. Aridity becomes freshness, and dulness liveliness. The metamorphosis, on its smaller scale, is like what happens when Shakespeare takes a novel and fashions it into a play. In this respect—though perhaps not always in the higher quality of suggestiveness—Chaucer is one of the best of borrowers.

I cannot refrain from noticing here an example or two of perfect adaptation in the writings of a man whose chief claim to remembrance does not lie in his poetry. John Wesley, a scholar of a high order, and one to whom all art was but a handmaid to piety, knew well how to utilise the phrases of others, and to quote literature for his moral purpose. Thus, in his fine translation, or rather imitation, of Tersteegen[1]:

> Thou hidden love of God, whose height,
>   Whose depth unfathomed, no man knows,
> I see from far thy beauteous light,
>   Inly I sigh for thy repose;
> My heart is pained, nor can it be
> At rest, till it finds rest in thee,

[1] "Verborgne Liebe Gottes du."

the last two lines are a close rendering of a saying of
St. Augustine ; but they fall so exactly into their new
context that one is surprised to find, on looking up
Tersteegen's hymn, that they are not there.   Again,
in a hymn made up by piecing together fragments
from two or three Spanish originals, we light on the
lines :—

> Hence our hearts faint, our eyes o'erflow,
> Our words are lost, nor will we know,
> Nor will we think of aught beside,
> My Lord, my Love, is crucified.

This last line is taken direct from an epistle of Ignatius,
written when the saint was on the way to martyrdom ;
and comes to us steeped in all the memories of a man
to whom the love of Christ was so compelling that
it overcame all fear of ignominy, torture, and death.

With other poets the case is often otherwise.   The
royal rule is that of Cyrus—no one should confer a
benefit on the prince without receiving a greater in
return.   Milton and Virgil, in the very act of borrowing, more than repay the debt.   Dante, when *he*
borrows, is like the man in the parable : he hands
back the gold, saying, "Thy pound hath gained ten
pounds."   All these are men of affluence ; though
they borrow, they can do without the accommodation.
But there are many who borrow because of poverty,
and as a result are poorer than before.   *Their* allusions
run perilously near to plagiarism ; and what they have
seized is not rarely spoilt in the transit.

Pope, as has often been noted, was a perfectly
rapacious borrower.   We cannot, it is true, attribute
his transactions with the literary Jews to financial

embarrassment : but they are certainly due to his characteristic thrift. He saves up the ideas and words of others, as he saved up old letters, that he may write, when occasion offers, between the lines or on empty pages. His depredations have been tracked in all sorts of places ; and the utmost he does with his materials is to reduce them to an epigrammatic form. Scores of examples may easily be gathered from any annotated edition : one may be added here.[1] One of the best-known couplets in the *Essay on Man* runs thus :—

> The spider's touch, how exquisitely fine !
> Feels at each thread, and lives along the line.

This is taken, and condensed, from Sir John Davies's *Nosce Teipsum :*—

> Much like a subtile spider, which doth sit
> In middle of her web, which spreadeth wide :
> If aught do touch the utmost thread of it,
> She feels it instantly on every side.

I do not think, when we note the allusions of Pope, that we feel quite the spider-like thrill which rewards us when we mark an allusion of Milton or Virgil : they are of a lower order, and appeal to a duller nerve in our mental system.

When we turn from Pope to Pope's admirer, Byron, we see, in my opinion, a further decline. His sources, says John Nichol, have been found in Rousseau, Voltaire, Chateaubriand, Beaumarchais, Swift, and a score of others ; and his descriptions are often taken from the notes of other travellers. "Like the rovers before Minos, he was not ashamed of his piracy."

---

[1] I have noticed this in another essay.

But a little shame he would have done well to feel, for his buccaneering expeditions were undertaken to fill an emptying purse, and often failed to bring home gold. He robbed the poor as well as the rich, and sometimes did not know how pitiful a loot he had gathered. Thus, in the third canto of *Don Juan*, the list of wares which formed the merchandise of Haidee's "piratical papa" includes :—

> A monkey, a Dutch mastiff, a macaw,
> Two parrots, with a Persian cat and kittens,
> A terrier too, which once had been a Briton's.

All these are mentioned, in the same order, by Lady Mary Wortley Montagu in a letter to her daughter Lady Bute (June 20, 1758) ; and the famous saying, "Man's love is of man's life a thing apart ; 'tis woman's whole existence," is from the eighteenth chapter of *Corinne*. The opening of the poem, "I want a hero, an uncommon want," reproduces a verse from Casti's *Novelle*. Much of the apostrophe to the Ocean in *Childe Harold* is again from *Corinne ;* "La mer reparaît telle qu'elle fut au premier jour de la création" ; and Harold himself, it has been noticed, is nothing but Madame de Staël's Nevil in varied conditions. Scraps of Lucretius and Horace, mingled with bits from authors of no reputation, diversify the Childe's pilgrimage, and lend the poem a curious aspect. And similarly with Scott's mimicries of *Christabel*. They do indeed direct out thoughts to the original, but only that we may feel what prentice-work they are. Far better not to have provoked the inevitable comparison. The Ethiop's ear is pleasanter to look at without the rich jewel.

We thus descend imperceptibly to the vast crowd, the *servum pecus*, of bad borrowers, pickers and stealers, ending with such men as Robert Montgomery, who steal and mar what they have stolen; and we reach the conclusion that the best borrowers are those who have abundance of their own; the great capitalists who, having large possessions, can make use of their loans from others.

Chapter IV

MEN's motives, at the best of times, being mixed, it is often very hard to decide what has led them to indulge in even so trifling a habit as allusiveness. Each individual allusion may have several motives, some of them apparently inconsistent with the others. But, with a due appreciation of our fallibility, and with the recognition that we shall never exhaust the mentality which has inspired the perpetration of the mildest literary theft, we may endeavour perhaps to discuss a few of the inducements which may have led to the crime.

A quotation may be adopted as a subterfuge ; you may shelter yourself under the authority of another author when you do not wish to face entire responsibility in your own person. When Carlyle quotes a blasphemy of Henry IV of France, and then adds, "By the same oath, charged to His Majesty's account, I think he was right," he was doing on a small scale what many writers do on a large. I remember a man who, when taken to task for using the contemptuous expression "Rats" in answer to an argument, excused himself by the ingenious assertion that he was merely quoting from the *Pied Piper of Hamelin*. Some years ago, a Member of Parliament told his opponents that they were "damned fools." When called to order, he declared that the phrase was a quotation, and that he had really inclosed it between inaudible inverted

44

commas. Though unable to state precisely which
author, out of the myriads who had employed the
phrase before him, he had in mind at the moment, he
yet seemed honestly to believe that the inverted
commas, had they been heard, would have justified
him completely. Chaucer, five hundred years earlier,
employed a not dissimilar device. He would not for
a moment, he assures us, have *himself* used the horrible
expressions of the Miller or the Summoner ; he is far
too gentlemanly. But as the reporter of their somewhat homely speeches he is constrained to be exact.

> But first I pray you of your curteisyë,
> That ye narette it not *my* vileinyë,[1]
> Though that I playnly speke in this materë,
> To tellë yow hir wordës and hir cherë ;
> Whoso shal telle a tale after a man,
> He moot reherce, as ny as ever he can,
> Everich a word, if it be in his chargë,
> Al speke he never so rudëlichc and largë.

"No, the 'vileinye' is not mine," says Chaucer,
"but that of the man whose words I am quoting."
Many another has salved his conscience in Chaucerian
fashion. A passage of Shakespeare, or a Miltonic
description of a devil, has served abusive orators
before now with the means of bespattering their
enemies and yet escaping the consequences. Even
Cicero, in his attack on Antony—though he certainly
allowed himself plenty of liberty to abuse his enemy
in his own name—hides himself once or twice behind
the shield of a "poeta nescio quis." The device is like
like that of a dramatist who expresses opinions, too

[1] i.e. vulgarity.

dangerous to be openly professed, by the mouth of characters in his plays whom he can plausibly disavow at any time.   Shakespeare himself, if Coleridge is to be believed, repeatedly acted thus.

Should your own opinions needs buttressing, or if it is desired to gain some attention for them which your own name is not illustrious enough to ensure, it is often worth while to point out that some great man, either actually or in appearance, agrees with you. You may *begin* your appeal by remarking that Dante, Goethe, or Wordsworth has said so and so ; this may help to break down the barrier of initial indifference which your readers may have set up against you.   Or, after launching a number of more or less dubious statements on the waves of prejudice, you may *conclude* by saying, "Whether or not this is true, at any rate this or that great man agrees with me ; for, as he says in such and such a place—" and here follows your quotation.   The advantage here is that as you are not the actual writer of the passage quoted, you may slide in a good deal more than you would otherwise have dared even to insinuate ; and, if the quotation is artfully chosen, you may perhaps get your readers to assent to a good deal more than you have proved. This is a device not infrequently adopted by public speakers, essayists, and lecturers ; they often end with a sounding passage which, purporting merely to *sum up* what they have said, in actual fact skilfully makes two and too add up to five.   I recall a very forcible peroration of this kind in one of Mr. Joseph Chamberlain's earlier Radical speeches.   After dwelling eloquently on the hindrances to useful legislation caused

by those who toil not neither do they spin, he ended
with the lines of Longfellow :—

> There is a poor blind Samson in this land,
>   Shorn of his strength, and bound in bonds of steel,
> Who may, in some grim revel, raise his hand,
>   And shake the pillars of this Commonweal.

The effect was electrical. No one wished to shake
the pillars of the commonweal, nor did Chamberlain.
But everyone in the audience felt somehow that he
had the strength of Samson, that he had been enchained
by tyranny, that he would break his bonds, and, like
Lear, "do such things—what they were he knew not."
Those few who recognised the passage—the papers
next day put it down to Tennyson—recalled how
Longfellow's prophecy was fulfilled ; how Samson
had raised his hand and the pillars of the great Republic
had been shattered ; and they would, for the moment,
imagine that they in England would win a victory
like that of Lincoln and the North ; but even those
who knew nothing about the verse at all would be
convinced that something great would happen, and
that they would bear their part in it. This is the
triumph of the quotation thus employed. In a gentler
style John Bright's Biblical reminiscence was equally
effective. Telling his Rochdale fellow-citizens why he
had refused office, he reminded them of the story of
the Shunammite woman, who, when Elisha said,
"Shall I do aught for thee with the King ?" replied,
"I dwell among my own people." Nothing could
have assured Bright's friends more strongly that, with
all his fame, he was of them and would remain with
them. And, like Chamberlain, he had kindled in

them a flame more intense than any other words, even of his own, could have done. It was as if Bright were reinforcing his decision with the hint that it was adopted in obedience to a Divine command.

Or, on the other hand, you may quote, with indignation or scorn, pointed perhaps with a touch of parody, a passage which expresses an opinion you detest. "This," you may say, "is what our adversaries hold, and this is the way they put it." Your parody may be a Swift-like distortion, or a mild twist : it may be uttered with a smile, or come forth with gnashing of teeth. If Samuel Butler is right, there is more than one such parody of the *Iliad* in the *Odyssey*, the "authoress" of which was irritated by the masculine arrogance of Homer's tone. Thus, in that exquisite passage of the sixth Book of the *Iliad*, Hector parts from Andromache with the words, "War is the business of men, and mine above all. As for thee, get thee back to the spindle, and bid thy maidens ply the task of women." But in the *Odyssey* we have a somewhat clumsy rebuke of Telemachus to his mother, bidding her return to the house, and mind her spinning and weaving : "*Talk* shall be men's business, and above all mine."[1] This is a sudden and unexpected sarcasm on the heroes of the *Iliad*, who certainly spend more time in haranguing than in fighting.

I know no better example of the Swift-like quotation than Job's bitter travesty of the eighth Psalm.[2] His "comforters" have rasped his nerves and fretted his

[1] Odyssey, i. 356. It should be noted that Aristarchus cut out the passage.
[2] Job vii. 17.

spirit beyond bearing with their slavish repetitions of worn-out maxims : and he bursts out in not unnatural frenzy. The pious Psalmist has wondered at the condescension of God, who has made the heavens with his fingers, and yet vouchsafes to be mindful of man, and to visit the son of man. "Ay," retorts the tormented Job, "What is man, that thou shouldst trouble to plague him, and fret him every moment ? If he is so little, why not let him alone ? Why set me up as a target, and plague me for thy sport ?" The God who can find enjoyment in chasing a helpless insect, or in harassing a withered leaf, may be great in power, but he is not great in soul.

In like but less intense manner, William Watson, to whom Kipling's Imperialism was utterly detestable, answered the *Recessional*. He quotes "Lest we forget" in sad irony, and points out that the British Empire was won, as has been said, in a fit of forgetfulness— but forgetfulness of God. In like manner also, I have heard the catch-phrases of unbelievers—Spencer's "conformity to environment" or Matthew Arnold's "something not ourselves which makes for righteous-ness"—quoted in the pulpit with clerical disdain, and then demolished with ecclesiastical eloquence. De Quincey, quoting the common saying that Pope's plume of distinction was "correctness," asks "Correct-ness in what ? " and then proceeds to give half a dozen examples in proof of Pope's amazing inaccuracy.

The advantage of such a method lies in this, that the passage quoted, being itself but a clinching epigrammatic summary of the opinions you detest, lays itself open, inevitably, to piecemeal demolition.

Being short, terse, and unqualified, it has all the weaknesses of a generalisation, and a few exceptions can easily be found. It is a much simpler task to meet this brief unguarded statement than to answer the long, consecutive, and cautious argument the conclusions of which it roughly gathers up into a few striking phrases. Thus, for example, the Benthamite slogan "The greatest happiness of the greatest number," has been again and again triumphantly dissected by people who would find it very hard to refute the laborious reasoning by which Bentham defends, explains, and limits it. I am no Marxian; but I am always a little annoyed when the Marxian principles are first assumed to be completely represented by some well-known Marxian phrase, and then contemptuously dismissed. It is a very old device: it was used, with disastrous effect, against Euripides by his enemies. He had allowed one of his characters, in a play, to utter the sentence, "My tongue hath sworn it, but my heart is free"—a saying, in its context, not only harmless but truistic. None the less, it was seized upon with avidity, ascribed not to Hippolytus but to Euripides himself, and repeated with wearisome iteration in order to disparage not merely the poet but his friends as well. All students of Greek know how Aristophanes delighted, in his comedies, to quote a few lines from the *Telephus* or the *Iphigenieia*, and by a juggler's twist make them mean what they had never been intended to mean. And the system has been pursued down to our own time. Asquith's innocent "Wait and see" was used by unscrupulous partisans against him until repetition at last blunted its edge.

Haldane's confession that "Germany was his spiritual[1] home" was a mere statement of the truth—he had been a pupil of the illustrious Lotze—but it was distorted with fatal results : we lost the services of one of the greatest war-ministers we ever had, and the country incurred the lasting disgrace of shameless ingratitude.

A slightly different use of the quotation as an engine of malice is that employed by the enemies of a still greater public benefactor than Haldane. The vigorous phrase "he makes the worse appear the better cause" was not Socrates' own. But it summed up very neatly and effectively what his enemies wished to believe about him, and was dexterously applied by his accusers at his trial to the perversion of justice. Without a short and sharp phrase like that, it is very likely that Anytus and Meletus might have failed to move the judges. A full and honest report of a single one of the philosopher's dialogues, fairly listened to, would have secured his acquittal. In a still better known trial the actual words of the accused, reported verbatim, and yet false because reported without their explanatory context, led to the most infamous condemnation in the history of the world.

More often, however, especially in written works, the quotation or allusion is inspired by more obscure motives. It starts to the mind, almost unbidden, as a neat ornament, as a forcible continuation of what you have just been saying, as a pleasant variegation of your style. It may spring from a mere schoolboy vanity : you can startle with a touch of cleverness.

[1] i.e. Intellectual, for Haldane was thinking of the German *geistig*— an untranslatable word.

Thomas Mozley, in his *Reminiscences*, tells how he was once at school drawing, very badly, a map of the world. A boy came up, glanced at the performance, and uttered the Homeric tag,[1] μὰψ, ἀτὰρ οὐ κατὰ κόσμον. Mozley says that he would have given a good deal to be able to make such a pun on the spur of the moment. Similarly, when Calverley, seeing how his own athletic feats were too much for his lazy friend James Payn, remarked "The labour *we* delight in physics Payn," there was nothing in his mind but a boylike delight in the aptness of the Shakespearean line to a new situation, combined perhaps with pardonable pleasure in his own ingenuity. Many of Burke's conversational puns, censured for frivolity by Dr. Johnson, were of this light and airy kind. There are many literary ones like them. One of the earliest I know may possibly be reckoned in this class. It occurs in so sombre a book as Ecclesiastes.[2] "Go thy way, eat thy bread with joy, and drink thy wine with a merry heart, for God hath already accepted thy works. *Let thy garments be always white ; and let not thy head lack ointment. Live joyfully with the wife whom thou lovest all the days of the life of thy vanity.*" Here is a verse from no less an epic than the Babylonian *Descent of Ishtar*. I do not see how Koheleth can have expected it to be recognised : at any rate it had to wait for recognition for perhaps two thousand years. Just possibly, he may have hoped that its verse form, in the middle of his own prose, would betray it *as* a

[1] "Poorly done and not in due order" : but the boy meant "maps, but not resembling the world."
[2] ix. 7.

quotation from somebody or other : but even this
is doubtful. I should imagine that it came quite
unbidden into his mind ; that he felt it, half unconsciously, to be suitable in that place, that it slid naturally
from his pen to the papyrus, and that at the very
utmost he would murmur to himself when he saw it
on the page, "That is something good." Thousands
of quotations and allusions have crept into literature
in just this quiet fashion.

It is not easy to acquit Cicero of vanity whatever he
was doing. Whether crushing Catiline, or writing a
letter, or even repenting of his cowardice and vacilla-
tions, he was always conscious that nobody else could
have done it quite so wonderfully. His very follies
had the *cachet* of Marcus Tullius about them. When,
then, we notice the hundreds of quotations—half-
dozen lines from plays, truncated lines from the Greek,
single words—which crowd his letters to Atticus, we
know that he meant Atticus to recognise them, and
that he plumed himself upon them, however tiny they
might be. "See how I have the appropriate Greek
ready for any emergency, the right parallel from
Homer, the pat speech from Terence." No other
ancient author, assuredly, has half so many ; and
Atticus must have had a kindly ironical smile for them
as they came pouring out for his benefit. He knew
that his friend was as vain of his Greek *clichés* as of his
finest original invectives against Antony or his best
philosophical declamations. In one short letter
describing a visit of Caesar to him, there are ten Greek
words (some single ones hiding a quotation) and a
line from Lucilius. In the famous letter to Lucceius,

E

of which we know Cicero was specially proud, there
are references to Callisthenes, Pyrrhus, Polybius,
Xenophen, Epaminondas, Themistocles, Alexander,
Timoleon, Homer, Herodotus, and Naevius. Cicero's
Latin vocabulary was large enough, and his power of
using it unsurpassed : but he knew how to increase its
force by borrowing the words of others. You can
scarcely read three pages of him without seeing that
this very original author had learnt how to quote.

I am not sure that Cicero does not frequently use
these truncated lines and curtailed quotations, especially when writing to his keen-witted friend Atticus, as
kind of password or cipher. They are telegraphic
signals to one who knows : in the words which Gray
borrowed from Pindar, they are "vocal to the intelligent." So, when more formally used in books, they
are messages from the writer to the more alert among
his readers. "Dullards may not understand, but *you*
will" ; and the reader who does understand, is
flattered at this sign that his intelligence is recognised.
He is in the secret with the author ; the two have a
language in common unknown to the vulgar. Whether
Cicero was thinking thus or not, Gray certainly was,
as his motto from Pindar shows. His *Progress of
Poesy* is a letter in code to those who have the key.
The first words, "Awake, Aeolian lyre," tell the instructed reader where to look, and the later verses
reproduce the "Aeolian" strain. To compare high
things with lower, this is like what happens in families
which have a "quote-book" known to all, and whose
conversation is garnished with allusions and phrases
bewildering to those who do not know it. Such

families can often speak in shorthand ; two words, even one word, may do as much effective work as whole sentences, and elicit an immediate response of equal brevity. I have known such families, and it has been quite astonishing to see the multitudinous uses to which a single book may be turned, or the varied significance that can be wrung out of a few phrases snatched from their original setting, and tossed to and fro like a conjurer's ball. A similar pleasure may be gained in reading certain allusive writers, who toss to you their rapid and careless allusions, rejoicing if you catch them, and expecting you to follow them out into their most subtle associations.[1] It is brevity like this that is often the soul of a very delightful kind of wit.

---

[1] A good example may be found in Sir William Rothenstein's reminiscences. Supping in a hot room with Ellen Terry, he murmured, "By the living Jingo." Instantly Ellen Terry replied, "So am I," got up, and opened the window. She had seen the allusion to a passage in the ninth chapter of the *Vicar of Wakefield*, which my reader may look up for himself.

Chapter V

THERE is scarcely a book of any importance or reputation—at least in that domain which De Quincey calls the "Literature of Power"—but will supply the reader with numerous examples in illustration of the principles which I have briefly touched on. We can often mark off a writer, and put him into his class, by noting the kind of quotations and allusions in which he indulges : nor less certainly can we detect the kind of readers to whom he makes his appeal. The "fit audience" which Milton desired for *Paradise Lost* is plainly discovered by the multitudinous echoes of the classics and the Scriptures scattered throughout the poem, without an understanding of which it cannot be duly appreciated. And as—to use an aphorism which will turn up again in a moment—"abeunt studia in mores," not merely the scholarship and mental culture of Milton's fit audience, but its character also, lie bare to the view. It must have, at least in some measure however small, the Miltonic loftiness, grandeur, self-reliance, and scorn of the vulgar. Similarly, as in looking at a man's library and noting what books are well-thumbed and annotated, we learn what the man is, so, in marking an author's allusions and quotations we learn, to a very remarkable extent, what the author is. They tell us which books he has "thumbed to rags," and therefore tell us what he himself is like. Moreover, the way in which he uses them, for ornament, for display, for business-ends, bewray him as the Galilean speech bewrayed St. Peter.

It may perhaps be worth while to choose, as examples of what may be revealed in this fashion, two writers of comparable genius and intellect, but belonging to different ages, writing with different ends in view, and making their appeal to different readers, yet not so dissimilar that comparison is futile. Francis Bacon and Edmund Burke were both statesmen, both men of vast and comprehensive powers. Both—though one of them was an Irishman—may be called English. Both were rhetoricians of the highest order, and both had extraordinary gifts of illustration ; they could throw light upon a subject by images drawn from regions of thought and knowledge at first sight unpromising. Both had human faults ; and yet it is but justice to say that both, though in unlike manner, were filled with enthusiasm for the betterment of mankind, and have been recognised by mankind as "Mehrer des Reichs," enlargers of our mental or moral domain. Both were students of law, and one a practising lawyer. But whereas Bacon, in his endeavour to gain a hearing, had to write for the great and powerful of *his* time, that is for King James and his ministers, Burke, in order to influence the world, had to speak to the members of Parliament, then the real rulers of his country. Bacon, again, was aiming at the "emendation of the intellect" and the "improvement of the sciences" ; Burke's desire was to influence the course of practical affairs. Hence Bacon's books are often as it were letters to individuals ; Burke's are, at least in intention, adapted to the minds of politicians banded in groups. If Bacon can persuade the King, he has attained his end ; if Burke can gain over a majority of the House of Commons, or of those to whom the members owe their seats, *his* end will be attained. Both use all the devices at their command for conciliating, pleasing, and convincing their hearers; their styles, their rhetorical devices, their *quotations*, are such as they imagine will promote their purposes and win over their audience to willing alliance with them. Much might be written on the degree of success or failure which attended their efforts to adapt their general way of writing to their purpose. For us, at the present moment, it will be enough to consider the kind of quotations they used, and the manner in which they used them.

Let us then take a glance at Bacon's *Advancement of Learning*, which is in form a letter to King James. There is, of course, plenty of direct and almost nauseous flattery; much eulogy of the King's largeness of capacity, strength of memory, penetration of judgment, and facility of elocution. But there is also plenty of the more refined blandishment shown in making literary allusions which the learning of the King will, as is implied throughout, always be able to catch. James's oratoric skill calls up a reminiscence of the words used by Tacitus of Augustus's "profluens, et, quae principem deceret, eloquentia"; his universality reminds Bacon of Hermes Trismegistus; and his mental powers suggest the phrase of Solomon, that "the hearts of kings are unsearchable."

When we pass to the main theme of the book, we notice at once that the quotations are usually full and formal, assigned to their originals, and dressed out so that they cannot fail to be recognised. Even the printer is called in to aid the reader ; they are given in italics so that the first glance may show that they are not Bacon, but Plato, Socrates, or Livy. "Knowledge is no more *Lumen siccum*, whereof Heraclitus the profound said *Lumen siccum optima anima*" ; "Seneca speaketh : *Quidam tam sunt umbratiles, ut putent in turbido esse quicquid in luce est*" ; Machiavel said, "*That the kingdom of the clergy had been long before at an end, if the reputation and reverence towards the poverty of friars had not borne out the scandal of the superfluities and excesses of bishops and prelates.*"

Again, the quotations are generally employed in order either to buttress Bacon's own opinions with the authority of some great name, or to provide brief texts representing opinions which he hopes to overthrow. They are business-like, utilitarian, informed with a practical purpose : resembling rather the quotations of a barrister from the legal decisions of judges than ornamental appendages. It is but rarely that Bacon introduces a line from Virgil or Lucan to *diversify* his pages or lighten the inevitable heaviness of his general argument ; just as it is but rarely that the quotation appears without its imposing accompaniment of author and book. He is usually saying, "Some people think so and so ; but Titus Livius, who can hardly be wrong, holds a contrary opinion" ; "This may seem heretical, but I have the following passage of Holy Writ on my side to prove my orthodoxy." We know from Bacon's biographers that he was a diligent extractor of striking sentences or anecdotes from the authors he read. We should have known, without being told, that he kept commonplace books, and that he entered passages in them with a view to future use.

When we turn to Burke, we find things, as a general rule, very different. The quotations are not sought for; they occur. As Burke goes on his way, his thoughts crowding on his mind, a passage, which his memory happens to recall, strikes him as appropriate, and falls naturally into its place. Thus, in explaining why the Americans could endure commercial restrictions, he says, it was because they were used to such restrictions, so to speak, from childhood: "The Act of Navigation attended the colonies from their infancy, grew with their growth, and strengthened with their strength." This is a natural, almost inevitable, quotation; who does not feel that it came spontaneously into the mind of the orator, that he had not to turn up his Pope laboriously to find it? But the passage, as Burke uses it, is an adornment, an aid to stylistic force: it is not an *authority*. Again, when speaking of Lord Chatham, Burke can hardly help himself: the words of Lucan about Pompey recur to him of their own accord, and his pen, almost unurged by his mind, adds "clarum et venerabile nomen." Such reminiscences are found everywhere in those noble speeches: "the day-star of the English constitution had arisen in their hearts"; "no sea but what is *vexed* by their fisheries"; "he was then old enough *acta parentum jam legere*"; "they who are too weak to contribute to your prosperity may be strong enough to complete your ruin, *spoliatis arma supersunt*"; "you cannot persuade them to burn their books of curious science"; in all these, and in scores of others, the quoted phrases are inextricably woven into the texture of the style, and the allusiveness is an essential part of the force. Often, as we see, the effect is gained by a single word : the *vexed* sea is enough to refer us to the Bermoothes— a singularly apt reference when Burke is speaking of the West Indian trade of the Americans—and the *curious* science is enough to remind the alert reader of the magicians of Ephesus.[1]

A good example of the contrasting methods of the two great writers is found, remarkably enough, in their use of the very tag I mentioned above, the Ovidian saying, "Abeunt studia in mores."   Compare the way in which it is applied by Bacon in the *Advancement of Learning* with the way in which Burke uses it in the speech on *Conciliation with America.* "No doubt," says Bacon, "there be amongst learned men, as in other professions, of all temperatures ; yet so as it is not without truth which is said, that *Abeunt studia in mores ;* studies have an influence and operation upon the manners[2] of those that are conversant in them." This is, it is true, a much less formal and deliberate quotation than most of those which Bacon gives us ; and it is given still more simply in the *Essay of Studies ;* but it does not slide in as easily or naturally

---

[1] At times, I venture to hold, Burke carries his allusions into full quotations, when one word would have been sufficient. When he refuses to be drawn into the abstract question of the *right* of taxation, he compares it to "the great Serbonian bog, betwixt Damiata and Mount Casius old, where armies whole have sunk." *Serbonian,* I think, would have been enough. Burke's quotations, like his arguments generally, are sometimes too elaborate. He "went on refining," and the audience went out to dinner.

[2] *Mores* is probably better represented by "character" than by "manners" ; but this does not affect my point.

as in the speech of Burke. Noting that the study of law, with all its virtues, has a tendency to make men rebellious, Burke says, "When great honours and great emoluments do not win over this knowledge to the service of the state, it is a formidable adversary to government. If the spirit be not tamed and broken by these happy methods, it is stubborn and litigious. *Abeunt studia in mores.* This study renders men acute, inquisitive, dexterous, full of resources. They anticipate the evil, and judge of the presence of the grievance by the badness of the principle. They augur misgovernment at a distance ; and snuff the approach of tyranny in every tainted breeze."[1] Here the quotation is not necessary to the argument ; it adorns, and so far as it enforces, it enforces not by adducing an authority but by starting in the reader a train of pleasant suggestions.

For Burke could rely on his readers. He knew they knew their Ovid, and he could be sure they would at once recognise the line, and follow it to its context. They had been brought up on the Latin classics, and could cap verses from the Augustan poets. But they knew them in a different way from that in which the contemporaries of Bacon knew them. To know them was the mark of a gentleman, and little more. To the men whom Bacon had before his eyes the Latin and Greek classics were still, as they were to the men of the Renaissance, all but inspired : their sentences were without appeal, and a quotation from them settled a question. To gain the assent of his readers, Bacon

---

[1] These last words are themselves a quotation—from Addison's *Cato.*

had no resource more certain than to find some saying of the classics which might seem to be on his side ; for his readers were still in the mental condition of Dante, who could refer to Livy as an historian without an error, or as the Schoolmen, who could silence opposition with a passage, possibly spurious, from Aristotle.   Burke, in a word, used a quotation to give pleasure, Bacon to conciliate hostility.

Not that the two methods do not sometimes approach : for hostility is often best conciliated by the giving of pleasure.   Thus, when Bacon, addressing King James, compares him and his predecessor, as patrons and devotees of learning, to Castor and Pollux, *Lucida sidera*, the Horatian allusion does the same work as Burke's comparison of the effect of Henry VIII's enfranchisement of Wales to the calm brought about by the same lucid deities :

> Simul alba nautis
> Stella refulsit,
> Defluit saxis agitatus humor,
> Concidunt venti, fugiuntque nubes.

Both James and the Parliamentary majority would tend to yield to the gentle flattery implied in the presentation of an allusion which they recognised.   Nevertheless, the fact remains that as a rule the quotations of Burke are what Cicero calls "lumina" or "insignia," decorations ; while those of Bacon, though so much more obvious, are essential to his design.   Substitute for Burke's quotations other words—you spoil the style but you do not affect his argument.   Cut out Bacon's quotations, and you destroy the whole force of his appeal to his readers.

Thus, then, the range of a writer's allusions, and the manner in which he makes them, provide us, as I said, with clear indications of the character both of himself and of his readers. The same could be shown by subjecting to a similar examination other authors, such as Fuller, Macaulay, Ruskin, De Quincey; and indeed few more pleasant exercises for a leisure hour could easily be found than such an examination. But this I leave to others, only venturing the conjecture that future literary historians may possibly be able to detect the limitations of our own age by noting the allusions which are *not* made by popular authors of to-day. Tacitus tells us that when Junia, the sister of Brutus, died, the Emperor forbade the effigies of Brutus and Cassius to be exhibited in the funeral ceremonies, but that they were only the more conspicuous by their absence. Similarly, when the future historian sees how few are the Biblical or Miltonic allusions in present-day writers, and compares them with the constant references in those of earlier centuries, he may draw conclusions, which we may hope will be mistaken, as to the ignorance both of authors and of their public. With the vast increase in the numbers of those who read, there has been a change in the style of those who write for them; and not least marked is the change in the kind of quotation in which the writers indulge. Many, indeed, whether from choice or from poverty, rarely quote at all. Whether this proves their extreme originality, or indicates that they have written without a preliminary course of reading, may be doubted.

Chapter VI

IT is a truth too often forgotten, and yet obvious on the least consideration, that every book has many authors. There is the so-called writer, and there are the readers, every one of whom contributes his share : it is the combination of these that makes the alloy we call "book." In few words, the noun book is a noun of multitude in another than the grammatical sense : its effect on every reader is, and must be, different from its effect on every other. This is because the mental equipment of each is different from that of his fellow, and it is impossible that the content of the book can impinge in the same way on minds of unequal and unlike content. We constantly notice, therefore, that what we call for convenience the same book, affects various readers with various emotions, ranging in certain cases from utter loathing or contempt to extreme admiration. A mathematician, prepared by his previous studies for his task, will welcome Salmon's *Conics* with delight, and call it "beautiful" : not so a Macaulay or a Dean Stanley. To Buckle, a lexicon was an object of affection, and every new one was opened with expectation ; to many people it is, at best, a mass of dull utility.

This has both its advantages and its disadvantages ; it is, at any rate, pretty certain that it is as well not to have too much monotony either in the external or in the intellectual world. If all the seas were ink a sea-voyage would lose some of its attraction : and if all books were appreciated equally, literary conversations might lose some of their zest.

In nothing are these differences manifested more strikingly than in the ways we judge the allusiveness of an author. To a man with wide and exact knowledge the allusions may appear childish and commonplace : to another recondite and over-learned. A man familiar for years with an out-of-the-way branch of study may quote easily and lightly from the Vedas or the epic of Gilgamesh ; another, having just started on Horace or Virgil, may try to show off by quoting verses that have been the common stock for two thousand years. To Bentley an allusion to Terentianus Maurus was hackneyed and stale, and a reference to Aelian's *Various History* so obvious as hardly to be worth making : while there are people to whom one made to *Alice in Wonderland* may seem ostentatious. "Don't air your history here," says a father in a novel I remember, when his son begins to talk about Napoleon and the battle of Jena : while another, with more justice, reproves his boy for venturing on so prodigious a piece of classical erudition as "Timeo Danaos et dona ferentes."

This last tag was vented at the dinner-table : and this suggests that a quotation may be pedantic in one place and natural in another. In the class-room "Timeo Danaos" might have earned approval from the master : at home, before the boy's sisters, the father was right to suppress it. An academic sermon may, or at one time might, be spiced with Latin : a country vicar had better stick to the vernacular ; and so a book designed for a cultivated audience may indulge in quotations that will not do in a book intended for popular consumption.

Again, the quotation must be accurate.   No one is bound to quote, but if he does quote, he should quote correctly.   Nothing did more harm to Ouida's reputation than her habit of using classical tags which the scholar saw through at once.   Thus, after proclaiming that one of her military heroes, despite the fact that he never opened a book, had more Latinity than most professors, she makes him repeatedly use the phrase "cui bono ?" as if it meant "What's the good ?"

It is plain, then, that an ignoramus may be a pedant : indeed pedantry is commoner in the ignorant than in the truly learned.   We must define pedantry not so much by reference to the effect of the quotation on the reader as by the motive of the writer ; and this can be discovered only, as a rule, by finding out the general character of the man.   If the learning slips out simply and almost unconsciously ; if it is worn lightly as a flower, and not with vanity, then however marvellous the erudition may be, there is no pedantry.   I do not think, for instance, that any competent judge would call Burton's *Anatomy of Melancholy* pedantic, though it contains more Latin quotations than any book except Lewis and Short's *Dictionary*, and though Burton is said to have carried off many tons' weight of literature from the Bodleian in order to cram it still tighter with learning.   If pedantry be rightly defined as knowledge out of place, then Burton is no pedant ; for, I imagine, we instinctively feel that his mind was the right tenement for knowledge, and his book the right store-room in which to stow it.   There may be some ostentation about the way in which he displays his treasures : but to me, at least, it always seems out-weighed by his manifest desire to give his readers pleasure.   He is a man who has gathered an enormous number of pictures, who has a natural pride in his possessions, but who delights most in showing his friends round and sharing their enjoyment.   "See that beautiful landscape," he seems to say ; "I picked it up at such a place : is it not wonderful, and have I not found the exact spot where the light will best fall on it ?"   No man ever, to a superficial glance, buried himself more completely beneath his furniture, yet somehow no one has ever reavealed himself more naively.   And the man revealed is one it is almost impossible not to like.   We accept cheerfully from him what we would reject from anyone else.

Much the same, *mutatis mutandis*, may be said of Thomas Fuller.   But our feelings towards Fuller are different from those aroused by Burton.   We are grate-ful to Burton for introducing to us a thousand passages we have never seen before : whereas to Fuller we are grateful for giving familiar passages a new and quaint turn.   His quotations are easily tracked ; they are mainly from the Bible ; but his eccentric humour has twisted them round so that they look new.   "It was laid to the charge of Bishop Wulfstan that he could not speak French ; but this is no essential quality in a bishop as St. Paul describes him in the Epistle to Timothy.   Sure I am that he could speak the language of Canaan." Bishop Herbert of Thetford was "a flatterer and a simoniac"; but he "purged away his guilt by a pilgrimage to Rome, as the leprosy of Naaman was washed away in Jordan."

Whether the Elizabethan dramatists are to be charged with pedantry for the vast number of Latin tags which they use, is hard to decide. Most of them were Latin scholars, and would certainly have these tags at their fingers' ends, so that they often slip out naturally and easily; they are the overflow of full minds. We must remember also that the gentry sitting on the stage were also Latin scholars, and would take every quotation instantaneously; while the groundlings would be consoled ere long with *ex tempore* vulgarities from the mouth of the clown. "Enter clown, who can say *anything*," is a stage-direction of 1605. The difficulty, then, of the playwrights was that which so often confronts orators—an audience of very various degrees of intelligence; and they met it in the only possible way, by appealing now to one part of the audience and now to another. They would rely also on the skill of the actors, who often attain remarkable success in making the crowds *think* they understand the words, while they really understand only the gestures.[1] Every now and then the Latin is astonishingly appropriate and suggestive. As John Addington Symonds remarks, Faustus's "O lente, lente, currite noctis equi," in his last terror-struck speech, borrowed from Ovid's *Amores*, is, in the mouth of a scholar, and at such a moment,

[1] I have sometimes watched audiences listening entranced to some of Shakespeare's hardest speeches. It is certain that the words are unintelligible : but the people are quite unconscious of the fact, and imagine them simple.

the very height of pathos—to those who understand.
"By an exquisite touch of nature—the brain involun-
tarily summoning words employed for other purposes
in happier hours—Faustus cries aloud the line which
Ovid whispered in Corinna's arms."[1]   Here there can
be no suspicion of pedantry ; the appropriateness is
such that it is an impertinence even to offer a defence.
And the next lines, English, and intelligible to the
dullest, immediately make their appeal to universal
humanity—to the well-dressed lordlings, to the appren-
tines in their leathern aprons, and to the groundlings
standing on the bare earth and under the open sky.

It would appear that pedantry was very early noted
as ruining the charm of an allusive style.   We know,
for instance, that Pollio, the friend and patron of Virgil
was charged and apparently justly, with this fault.
The Roman critics speak of him as vain of his learning,
and as showing it off, even in his speeches, by constant
quotations from Ennius and Pacuvius ; which is as if
a barrister should adorn his addresses to the jury with
scraps of Chaucer.   Nor is this surprising : for we
know that as a critic he was severe on the writers of
his own time, and was a purist as to diction.   Even
in Livy he detected the provincialism of Northern
Italy : and he was always for cutting out anything
approaching the language of everyday conversation
from the works of his contemporaries—who, on their
side, often failed to understand what *he* had written.

There is indeed plenty of pedantry in Latin poetry,
even in its golden age.   When once it had been settled

---

[1] Wonderfully inverted by Juliet in her cry, "Gallop apace, ye
fiery-footed steeds."

that Roman literature must be an imitation of the
Greek, there was every temptation for the poets to
try to gain repute by clever mimicries ; and when the
more obvious sources had been well tapped, it was
inevitable that later writers should seek the more
obscure.   Pedantry spoils the real and powerful genius
of Propertius, who, though deeply in love with an
actual living woman, cannot help ransacking the worm-
holes of long-vanished days to find comparisons for
her beauty and her caprice.   It says much for the
vitality of Cynthia and the passion of Propertius that
she is still alive after all these antiquarian doses.   He
calls himself a Milanion, hurt with the indifference of
Atalanta : but he cannot speak even of Atalanta by her
ordinary name ; she is the daughter of Iasus.   Cynthia
spends too much time on dress : "it was not thus that
Phoebe and Hilaeira fired the breasts of Castor and
Pollux ; no, nor thus that the daughter of Evenus[1]
became the cause of contention between Apollo and
Idas."   "As the Gnosian maiden lay wilting on the
abandoned shores, while the Thesean keel was fading
in the distance, as the Edonian,[2] wearied with the
dance, sank down by grassy Apidanus, so seemed
Cynthia to me, as she rested her head on her waver-
ing hands."   No wonder Dean Merivale says that
Propertius got his learning from dictionaries—though
dictionaries there were none in his day.   You feel that
he *must* have looked all this up in some Lemprière.
And yet with all this frigidity and ostentation, there are

---

[1] Marpessa : the theme of a beautiful poem by the now despised
Stephen Phillips.
[2] A Bacchanal.

love-passages in his poems as simple and direct as a song of Burns. The fatal strength of fashion—no poet could then gain a hearing unless he loaded every rift with Hellenic mythology—was too much for him. He was like those poets of ours who could not call a girl by her English name, but must denude her of all reality by dubbing her Chloe, Lalage, or Chloris.

Much worse than Propertius is Persius, and he is without either Propertius' redeeming genius or his underlying sincerity. He is for ever quoting, and distorting his author ; for ever alluding, and darkening his allusions by words with too much knowledge in them. He was a young man, hardly out of the schoolroom, and extravagantly vain of his recently-acquired scholarship. His chief model is Horace : but where Horace had been simple and natural, Persius is always twisted and affected. Whatever in his original slips easily into its place, he drags in by force : whatever is plain in its neatness he makes obscure and turgid. A glance at the hundreds of parallels collected by the commentators will show the kind of thing. I will give but one example. The Pythagoreans represented the path of life by the letter Y : the stem standing for the untutored innocence of childhood, the broad and easy branch for the way of vice, the thin and hard one for the way of virtue. How does the young Stoic remind us of this symbolism ? "The letter which spreads its Samian ramifications has shown thee the steep path which rises with its right-hand track." This is not the writing of a poet with his eye on the subject ; it is the writing of a boy who wishes to be thought clever.

Something all too like Persius may be found in our own day, and particularly in what has in sundry places passed muster as poetry. Mr. I. A. Richards has declared that all poetry is an act of communication; but of much modern verse the opposite would seem to be true; it is an act of obscuration. The outside appearance of the poem would seem to be summoning us to an audience; but when we approach the man we find he is speaking in a language unintelligible to us. This is worse in a poet than in anyone else; for every true poet is an individual, and has something individual to tell us; something of his own, to elevate, to console, to strengthen, or merely to please. If we cannot understand an historian, we can get the history, in some form, from another. If we cannot understand a book of economics, we can try another economist. But a poet's communication is unique; it is of himself, or it is nothing. And, among poets, this is especially true of lyric poets—by far the largest class at present. Yet it is hardly too much to say that very many modern lyrists make their poems as obscure, by dint of their hidden allusions, as if they were written in Hebrew. This is ungenerous of them. Obviously their personalities are worth communicating, or they would not be poets. Then why do they mock us as if they were about to bestow a liberal largesse; and when we pick up their coins, why do we find them of a foreign mintage, uncurrent in our land? It is really too bad. We buy, beg, or borrow one of these epoch-making volumes, in the hope of finding there something that may do for us what *In Memoriam* did for our grandfathers; and we do indeed find paper with print on it ; but what it means we cannot tell. High thinking, we are sure, must be there ; but the plain speaking, which would make the thoughts so beneficial to us, is absent. We are like the caravaners in the Book of Job, deceived by the mirage : "We are ashamed because we had hoped."

If English poets, and poetesses, thus disappoint, American are still more disappointing. The Transatlantic "Modernist" school seems to have set before itself as its one aim that it shall not be understanded of the people. Its very title-pages—for example, "is five"—need an interpreter : and as for its text, we are in the position of the Ethiopian eunuch, except that the Philip rarely appears. It quotes, but we know neither that it is quoting, nor whom it is quoting from ; it alludes, but its allusions are caviare even to the instructed ; and when it uses its own words, they mean one thing in one line and another in the next.

I must however make a confession. Not to violate my own principles, I must lay no claim to an erudition I do not possess. I have never read a single volume of any one of these authors completely through, and scarcely three dozen individual poems. My knowledge of them is derived from magazines, from a chilly dip into certain writers and a hasty rush to the shore, from hearing a few recitations, and from that work of Miss Laura Riding and Mr. Robert Graves, to which I have already referred. I may well be told that with such a slender equipment I am incompetent to judge. I can only reply that, inadequately as I have studied the subject, I have learned, in whatsoever state of ignorance I am, therewith to be content.   Nor

shall I burden the reader with examples.   One, from
Mr. Cummings, I have already given : and that the
reader will probably find sufficient.   But I may perhaps
point out that this sort of thing, new as it claims to be,
has not even that distinction.   It is, as might be
expected by all who know anything of literary history,
as old as vanity itself.   Something not unlike it is
known as Góngorism, and Góngora was born in
1561.   Annoyed, as some say, by the failure of his
simpler verses, he tried to gain repute by contorting
his style, and at any rate, made his *name* famous.
I take a specimen from Mr. David Hannay's *Later
Renaissance :* a "poem" on Pyramus and Thisbe, which
Mr. Hannay thus literally translates :—

> Pyramus they were and Thisbe,
> Those who in verse made polished
> The Licentiate Naso,
> Maybe snub, maybe beak,
> To leave the sweet white
> Lamentably dark
> Of that which, tomb of silk,
> Was of the two feather-heads
> Mulberry which gave them shelter,
> And was condemned at once,
> If by the Tigris not in root
> By the lovers in fruit.

Here the reader may be glad to learn that "made" in
line 2, goes with "to leave" in line 5, and is the verb
to the subject "Naso" ; while the whole passage, as
interpreted by an admiring commentator, means that
the mulberry was not rooted up by the Tigris, but was
discoloured by the blood of the lovers.   Even
Góngora, as Mr. Hannay points out, was not the first

in the field. He had been anticipated by the Icelandic court-poets, whose riddles, "kennings," and inversions of the natural order of words, to say nothing of their mythological allusions, are not less difficult, and far more ingenious, than any conundrum of Mr. Cummings. But we can go yet further back. The last chapter of *Ecclesiastes* is as obscure as the works of these moderns, but, unlike them, repays the trouble of unravelling. Its phrases, obviously borrowed from earlier writers, *can* be translated into ordinary language. The *Cassandra* of Lycophron might teach a lesson to the most unintelligible of latter-day bards ; and, like their performances, owes its obscurity to the desire of showing off the recondite learning of the author— with this difference, that Lycophron's learning, though largely useless and trivial, was *real*.

Chapter VII

No maxim is better justified by experience than the Delphian "Nothing in excess." All customs and fashions tend to extravagance, and what was once an occasional ornament enlarges itself into a burden. And then, for no assignable reason, the excess disgusts, and may be displaced in favour of an excess in the opposite direction.

I know nothing that so astonishingly illustrates extravagance in the small field of literature I am discussing as the prevalence, during some centuries, of the cento, which may be called quotation run mad. It exhibits every fault which the wise quoter ought to avoid : pedantry, ostentation, obscurity, over-ingenuity : and might well have been included by Addison, along with lipograms and acrostics, in his specimens of False Wit.[1] Yet as the vagaries of the human mind are often no less instructive than its normalities, it may be worth while to give a brief account of the cento in this place. Merely ingenious as it was, an exercise of toil and cleverness, it yet was practised by many minds far above the ordinary, and involved no more useless an expenditure of time than the making or solving of crossword puzzles. Some men indeed, who have left behind them works of original genius, amused their leisure with this quaint and curious sport.

[1] *Spectator*, Nos. 25, 58, 60.

Readers of Boswell will remember that wealthy and cultured gentleman, Richard Owen Cambridge, whose Twickenham villa, with its books and other treasures, more than once harboured Dr. Johnson, and whose serene and yet animated disposition called from Boswell the exclamation, "Fortunate senex." Cambridge read more than he wrote; but among his writings is the mock-epic the *Scribleriad*, in which the practisers of "false wit" are amusingly satirised. Scriblerus, the hero, is introduced to a country not unlike Ariosto's Moon, or Milton's Paradise of Fools, where literary triflers find themselves quite at home. There he meets

> Riddle, and Rebus, Riddle's dearest son,
> And false Conundrum, and insidious Pun;

the firm and compact Acrostics, in three fair columns, the uncouth Anagrams, the wedge-like Rhopalics, and all the other frivolities which, so early as the days of Domitian, earned the ridicule of Martial.[1] But the place of honour is reserved for the cento-makers:

> From different Nations next the Centos crowd,
> With borrowed, patched, and motley ensigns proud;
> Not for the fame of warlike deeds they toil,
> But their sole end the plunder and the spoil.

From this it is at once obvious what a cento is. Leaving aside the satirist's poetical metaphors, we may define it, with reference to the original meaning of the

---

[1] "Turpe est difficiles habere nugas,
    Et stultus labor est ineptiarum." (Mart., II, 86.)
A well-known Rhopalic is "Rem tibi confeci, doctissime, dulcisonoram": one in English would be: "Lines slowly lengthening successively, syllabically," every word one syllable more than its predecessor.

word (patchwork,[1] something stitched or pricked out)
as a composition in which every phrase is taken from
some previously-written work, and preferably from a
classic. A new poem, for example, may be made by
stitching together lines or half-lines from Virgil : such
a poem is a Virgilian cento. A good short definition
is given by Ausonius, who, about the year 370,
composed such a work by order of the Emperor
Valentinian. In the preface to this Wedding-Idyll,
Ausonius apologises for the sportive character of his
"opusculum," and, with a certain inconsistency, lays
down rules for those who wish to imitate him in his
frivolity. A cento is, says he, "de inconnexis con-
tinuum, de diversis unum, de seriis ludicrum, de
alieno nostrum"—continuity out of disconnectedness,
unity out of difference, jocosity out of solemnity, and
originality by means of plagiarism. A line, he adds,
may be appropriated whole or divided; but two
whole lines must never be taken in succession.

Though Ausonius does not always keep rigidly to
his own rules, the poem, while in places hardly likely
to please Victorian taste, yet extorts an unwilling
admiration by its cleverness. He thus addresses the
Emperor whose command had elicited the Idyll :—

Accipite haec animis, laetasque advertite mentes,
Tuque puerque tuus, magnae spes altera Romae,
Flos veterum virtusque virum, mea maxima cura,
Nomine avum referens, animo manibusque parentem :
Non iniussa cano.

In the margin, for the benefit of the Emperor, are
given the references to the despoiled passages. The

[1] We think of Locker-Lampson's elegant miscellany, *Patchwork*.

whole, in fact, might almost be the work of a schoolboy with a good verbal memory but not much taste,
who, set to do a prize Latin poem, produces a collection of tags from the classics.

At what time the cento proper, as thus defined and
exemplified by Ausonius, first arose, is uncertain;
indeed, while every fresh discovery in Egypt or
Babylon is proving the antiquity of some vaunted
novelty, it is futile to dogmatise. For all we know,
Pentaur's epic in praise of Rameses II's victory over
the Hittites may be a series of thefts from earlier poets.
But the reader will perhaps pardon me if I do not go
back beyond the Christian era. About 220 A.D.,
Tertullian, in his Prescription against ' Heresies,[1]
observes that all heresies are founded, or at least
partially supported, on centos taken from Holy Writ,
which is thus made to yield a sense very different from
the real one. "You see," he says, "in our own day,
composed out of Virgil, a story of a wholly different
character; the subject-matter being arranged according to the verse, and the verse according to the subject-
matter. Nay, Hosidius Geta[2] has completely pilfered

[1] He may have had in his mind, among other pieces of patchwork,
the forged "Epistle of Paul to the Laodiceans," which, as any one
may see by glancing at Lightfoot's *Colossians*, is a cento made up of
sayings from St. Paul's genuine letters, and jumbled heterogeneously
into a kind of order. But this forgery is quite harmless; even
Tertullian would have been hard put to it to find heresy in its clumsy
mosaic. It was, of course, written to satisfy curiosity as to the
Laodicean epistle mentioned in *Colossians*, iv, 16.

[2] Hence the theory of some that Ovid's lost tragedy of *Medea* was
a cento : *Hosidius* being taken as a scribal error for *Ovidius*, and *Geta*
as alluding to the honest poets residence among the Getae. But as
the ancients regarded the *Medea* as Ovid's best work, and as Hosidius'
performance is a wretched business we need not trouble to refute the
theory.

his tragedy of *Medea* from Virgil.   A near relative of
my own, among some leisure productions of his pen,
has composed out of the same poet the *Table* of Cebes.
On the same principle, those scribblers are called
Homero-centones who stitch into one piece, works
of their own from lines of Homer, out of scraps taken
miscellaneously from this passage and from that."
Similarly, he goes on, heretics stitch out of Scrupture
doctrines as little agreeable to its true sense as the
works of these poetasters are to the *Iliad*.   In any case,
this remark of Tertullian's shows that cento-making
was rife in the third century nor is there any reason to
suppose that Hosidius was the first in the field.   He
was assuredly one of the worst : for the five hundred
lines of his tragedy are as dull a performance as can
easily be found even in the leaden age of Roman
literature.

Of all blue-stockings one of the most famous, and
certainly the highest in station, was the learned
Athenais, who, in the year 421, married the Emperor
Theodosius II.   Under her father, Leontius, she had
studied every branch of literature and science then
known, and she had imitated the classical writers with
marked success.   She was a heathen, but in com-
pliance with the wishes of her imperial suitor, or rather
perhaps with the commands of the real ruler, his sister
Pulcheria, she accepted Christianity, and took the
name of Eudocia at her baptism.   Of her subsequent
career, her glory and her fall, those who desire to
learn may read in the stately periods of Gibbon.   She
aspired to be the Sappho of her time : but she con-
cerns us here solely for her reputed, but very dubious,

connection with what Gibbon calls "an insipid performance"—a cento from Homer, in which the *Iliad*
and *Odyssey* are very ingeniously compelled to yield a
life of Christ. Whatever the crimes of Eudocia, this
work is no longer reckoned among them. Scholars
seem agreed that it must be dated at least a century
later ; and some would lay it to the charge of Pelagius,
who flourished under Zeno about 474.

To read these verses is to receive a series of very
curious sensations. The classical scholar, as he sees
the familiar words of the old epic in their new setting,
fancies they have jumped out of their right pages and
are dancing before him in a kind of nightmare, like
Alice's pack of cards in Wonderland.

A set of Latin hexameters, formed out of Virgil, but
on a system somewhat less rigid than that of Ausonius,
describes certain events of Old and New Testament
times. This is beyond doubt earlier than the Homeric
cento of the pseudo-Eudocia : to judge from the
dedication to the Emperor Honorius, it must have
been written before 393. The author is said to have
been Proba Falconia, a distinguished Roman lady who
later, if we may believe a story handed down by
Procopius, proved herself a second Tarpeia, and
opened the gates of Rome, while the Senate slept, to
the conquering hosts of Alaric. But this story is
justly discredited by Gibbon and other scholars ; and
indeed the murder of Virgil is quite enough for one
woman without the addition of a Gothic massacre.
The poem fills fourteen closely printed columns in
Migne's monumental *Bibliotheca Patrum*, and, on a
rough calculation, is about as long as a book of the

Aeneid. It is appalling to think of the amount of labour that must have gone to the making of this huge trifle. The reader will probably be content with a small morsel, the description of the temptation of Eve : a passage which I sometimes idly fancy Milton may have seen :—

> Jamque dies infanda aderat per florea rura :
> Ecce inimicus atrox immensis orbibus anguis
> Septem ingens gyros, septena volumina versat ;
> Nec visu facilis, nec dictu affabilis ulli,
> Obliqua invidia ramo frondente pependit,
> Vipeream inspirans animam, cui tristia bella
> Iraeque invidiaeque, et noxia crimina cordi.
> Odit et ipse pater : tot sese vertit in ora,
> Arrectisque horret squamis, et ne quid inausum,
> Aut intentatum, scelerisve dolive relinquat,
> Sic prior aggreditur dictis, seque obtulit ultro.

The poem concludes with the Ascension of Christ, narrated in easily-recognisable words,

> I, decus, i, nostrum, tantarum gloria rerum,
> Semper honos, nomenque tuum, laudesque
>   manebunt.

The age of the Renaissance was not likely to leave the art of Cento-making untried. An age in which a clever *jeu de mots* might start an ecclesiastic on a career leading to the Papacy, and in which the discovery of the *Annals* of Tacitus ranked with the discovery of America, could not rest with printing the classics, but turned them inside out as well. The two Capilupi of Mantua, in the sixteenth century, produced more than one work of the kind, of which a Virgilian history of the Friars is the best known. From Stephen de

Pleurre's *Adoration of the Magi*, Cambridge, in the notes to the *Scribleriad*, quotes some lines. The Magi came,

> Munera portantes molles sua tura Sabaei,
> Dona dehinc auro gravia myrrhaque madentes.

Men of real distinction, as I have said, have sometimes sported in this fashion in their lighter hours. The learned Heinsius thus unbent the bow of Apollo ; and Alexander Ross, whose titles to fame are far more numerous than might be guessed from Butler's line, composed by way of recreation "the History of our Lord and Saviour Jesus Christ given in the words and verses of Virgil." According to Isaac D'Israeli, this poem was thought worthy of republication in 1769, a century after Ross's death. We are reminded of the freak of Thomas Tallis, a musician of the first rank, who yet once wrote an eight-part canon, which, if sung backwards, is precisely the same as if sung forwards.

I remember seeing in an old copy of the *Encyclopaedia Metropolitana*, an account of a more modern feat of the kind, a cento from many Latin authors written in honour of Nelson. The writer is unfortunately not named, but he was plainly a good scholar and an ingenious man. He had, it is true, lucky chances, but he availed himself of them with skill. Nelson's ship at Copenhagen was the *Elephant*, and, like Hannibal, he had lost an eye. This suggested to the writer an adaptation of Juvenal's line,

> Cum Gaetula ducem portaret belua luscum ;

and Nelson's Neapolitan title of Duke of Bronte gave

him an opportunity of working in a pun or two on the classical Bronte, thunder : while the hero's earlier service on board the *Agamemnon* was too obvious a gift of the gods to be let slip. Meanwhile, Napoleon, "unus homo quem Corsica misit," is standing at Boulogne like the shades on the strand of Styx, and stretching his hands in longing for the farther shore ; but

Fata obstant, tristique palus inamabilis unda.

Surveying this field, we notice that such merits as a cento may possess are just those which we have seen in the ordinary quotation or allusion. The theft must be recognised : the stolen jewel must fit neatly into its new setting ; and Ausonius' phrase, "ex alieno nostrum," might stand as the sufficient and exclusive definition of every satisfactory literary borrowing.

For the benefit of those who do not know Latin, I quote here from Layard's *Great Punch Editor*, a *jeu d'esprit* of Shirley Brooks, which will give them some idea of the feeling aroused in the minds of classical scholars by the verses of Ausonius or Falconia. I premise, however, that, while the ancient cento-writers contrived to make connected sense out of their pilferings, Shirley Brooks aimed at nothing more than to sound like sense for a moment or two. His whole production is seventy lines : I reproduce a small fragment.

Full many a gem of purest ray serene,
That, to be hated, needs but to be seen,
Invites my lays ; be present, sylvan maids,
And graceful deer reposing in the shades.

G

I am the Morning and the Evening Star,
Drag the slow barge or whirl the rapid car,
While wrapt in fire the realms of ether glow,
Or private dirt on public virtue throw.
How small, of all that human hearts endure,
The short and simple annals of the poor !
I would commend their bodies to the rack :
At least we'll die with harness on our back.
Remote, unfriended, melancholy, slow,
Virtue alone is happiness below,
As vipers sting, though dead, by some review ;
And now thou see'st my soul's angelic hue !

. . . .

Lorenzo, to recriminate is just :
Can storied urn, or animated bust
Survey mankind from China to Peru,
And see the great Achilles, whom we knew ?

———————

Note.—I have heard that the *Meghadhuta* of the great Indian poet, Kalidasa, is preserved for us entire and unaltered as embedded in the poetical works of Jinasena and others.   In Jinasena's work every stanza contains one or two lines from the *Meghadhuta*, the remaining lines being composed by Jinasena himself. Mr. Pathak, in his edition of *Meghadhuta*, says that the dovetailing of the two parts is so ingenious that no one, on reading it through, would have the slightest suspicion that it is not wholly Jinasena's.   But this process differs from cento-making, in that the portions of the original, if I have not misunderstood Mr. Pathak, are always given by Jinasena in their proper order ;   whereas the essence of the cento is that the order should be varied.

Chapter VIII

ALL books, more or less, are sins either of omission or of commission. The writers do that which they ought not to have done, and leave undone that which they ought to have done. The excuse for this little book has already been given in the preface : its sins are open, palpable, and confessed. Every reader will notice omissions—that is part of my design ; I wish rather to suggest than to teach. If the reader, in his subsequent studies, is led to notice more allusions than he would otherwise have done, to pause and consider whether they achieve their end or fail to achieve it, to observe whether they add to the force of a passage or diminish it, to mark whether they secure the brevity which is the soul of point, I shall be satisfied.

One thing is possible for all, and is indeed deliberately made easy for us by many authors—to watch the use of the quotation as a *text*. Very often, a passage from some classic writing, set out in typographical isolation at the beginning of a book, may obviate the necessity of a preface. Three lines, two, or even one, aided by the suggestions they arouse in the "intelligent," may do the work of pages. I know no one who has understood this art better than Shelley—though it is true that Shelley not seldom added a preface to his motto. What commentary on *Adonais* is more revealing than the couplet from Plato which heads that poem ? To choose but one of the services it does for us, it warns us to keep the philosophy of Plato in our minds as we read, and to seek our explanation of "Urania" in the *Symposium*. Or how could we gain deeper insight into the *Prometheus Unbound* than by reflecting on the profound meaning hidden in the line of Sophocles (which Shelley found in Cicero's *Tusculan Disputations*) "Audisne haec, Amphiarae, sub terra abdite" ? The inspiration of the poem, we learn, is drawn from the shades, and comes from consulting prophets in their tombs. The exquisite verses from Virgil, which introduce *Julian and Maddalo*, make that poem much more moving than it would be were they expunged.

In a different way, the motto of *Comus* betrays the mind of Milton : he has been, he tells us, over-persuaded to woo the Muses too early, before the long preparation which he deemed necessary for a work which posterity should not willingly let die. The Ovidian verses which usher in *Venus and Adonis* show that Shakespeare, like Milton, could despise popularity and seek the applause of the few ; while at the same time they point to the original from which he drew his Castalian draughts. I often think that if the early reviewers of *Endymion* had pondered over the line with which Keats introduced it, "The stretched metre of an antique song," they might have seen the poet's design more clearly, and might have judged the accomplishment more fairly.

More obvious, and more direct in their hints, are other mottoes that will occur to my readers. The essays of Addison and Johnson, the chapters of Scott's novels, are headed with a passage from the classics, or with an invented extract from an "Old Play" which was so old that it had never been heard of before Scott's time.   The object of Addison was often to show that his wisdom was but the wisdom of the ancients applied to modern uses ; somewhat in the fashion in which, as I have already said, the endless quotations of Bacon in the *Essays* or in the *Advancement of Learning* were meant to suggest that, despite his desire to provide a new organon for scientific discovery, the secret—had men but known how to make use of it—lay *perdu* in the past.   All things, was the implication, had been thought of by the ancients : we had but to translate their conceptions into modern ideas.   The purpose of Scott was slightly different, to attune the minds of his readers to what was coming, to set their expectations on the alert, for a satisfied expectation is always better than a surprise.   The story, we may say, has reached a certain point, and we are wondering what will come next ; here, in the motto of the chapter, is a hint as to its succeeding development :   can I guess the contents of this chapter from this tiny hint ?   You watch the story as it moves along, and, as the chapter proceeds, your mind is satisfied ; the hint has been enlarged according to your desire.   What chapter in all fiction was ever better mottoed than the one which is headed with

> Sound, sound the clarion, fill the fife,
>   To all the sensual world proclaim,
> One crowded hour of glorious life
>   Is worth an age without a name ?

You pause on that—the clarion is indeed sounded. You read on, and you hear the whole orchestra : the

words of Dundee are but a magnificent sermon on the
text. You end the chapter and turn back to the
beginning. The promise of those stirring words has
been nobly fulfilled. Your thoughts do not stop
there : you recall the story which Scott had been
remembering when he wrote the words—the story of
the choice set before Achilles, a long life and a forgotten one, or a short life with glory. This is the
acme of suggestive quotation.[1]

When a preacher takes a verse from the Bible,
explains it, amplifies it, and recurs to it, he provides a
yet simpler and commoner example of the same thing.
He is taking, in the vast majority of cases, the very
best, the perfect, expression of the thought which he
desires to enforce. Even if, *per impossibile*, he could
find words of his own that were in themselves better,
they could not come to the congregation with the
glamour of antiquity, the sanctions of religion, the
associations of childhood, the charm of familiarity
which yet retains reverence. His very first words are
those of authority, and not of scribal hesitation : they
claim and receive the hearing due to a hundred
memories. Happy is he if his own words, comment-
ing on them, do not minish and bring them low !

As one reads the writings of the ancients, one
reflects somewhat sadly how vastly they must be
weakened for us by our inability to capture the
associations they must have had for contemporaries.
An allusion once bright with vitality is now dimmed
or even dead. From the few which are still visible we

[1] It makes no difference whether the famous stanza is Scott's own
or borrowed.

feebly guess how many must have dissolved away. A dull scholium sometimes retains for us one that we should otherwise have known nothing of : but the effect is rather to make us realise our losses than to make us rejoice in the gain. All this should induce us to determine not to let slip those which *can* be kept and appreciated—that is, those in our own literature. Above all, let us not lose that knowledge of the Authorised Version, the great "quote-book" of the English-speaking races, without which thousands of passages in our classical writers must fall flat. That knowledge, alas, is rapidly dying out, and unless it be recovered, much of our best writing must perish with it.

Nothing can stimulate a good author more forcefully than the assurance that he can rely upon a public with a culture wide enough and deep enough to appreciate, without laborious explanation, the hints he gives : a public which is, in a sense, his own family, brought up on the same books, and ready to catch at once the allusions he makes to them. I have heard that the finest flower of Chinese education is that which, steeped in the Chinese classics, can convey in three pages of allusive writing, to the right readers, what would otherwise take thirty. We need not aim at such a consummation as this ; but we may well desire to create a public which will recognise and feel the allusions which our authors make within a certain well-defined range. "This much," the authors ought to be able to say, "I can be sure you will understand." When they are reasonably confident that the public has studied a certain number of great books, and knows them as the Greeks knew the Epic cycle or the

Mohammedans knew their Koran, writers will feel a freedom to which at present they are strangers, and which they certainly enjoy in far smaller measure than their predecessors of the Elizabethan, the Victorian, or even the Caroline age. Read, for example, the *Absalom and Achitophel* of Dryden. Is not the most striking thing about that poem the plain fact that Dryden could *trust* his public to catch all his allusions ? He knew that when he called Slingsby Bethell Shimei, his readers would not need to look up their Bibles to learn that Shimei had cursed the Lord's Anointed. Can a modern author be equally confident?

All this suggests a further point. In a wide aspect, allusion and quotation are a recognition that the world of literature is *one*. Here are no boundaries, no tariff-walls : nay, your purchases, like those of the prophet, are made without money and without price. The work of any great writer is his own property, but it is open to us all. Once written, it is a possession for ever and for everybody. You are at liberty to steal, if you can ; if, like Virgil, you can make off with the goods of Homer in the right fashion, and use them in the due manner. As the great preacher steals his text from Paul or John, and builds his great sermon on it, so you are at liberty to steal from Dante or Milton— if you are a thief on the grand scale. The sun's a thief, says Timon, and with his great attraction robs the vast sea. He has the right to do so : his pillage is huge enough to justify itself.

Lesser thieves are justified by the use they make of their booty. They cannot rob with Titanic magnificence : but they may pass if they annex what they really need, and employ it well. What they take must be capable of varied service, and they must put it to a service that is new and worthy. All things are permitted to them, though by no means all are convenient.

But the laws which limit these annexations are vague and hard to codify, as the penalties for their infringement are obscure and indefinite. No Justinian can draw them up with clearness and distinctness. Every theft is appraised on its own merits, and by a judge who has nothing but his own instinct to guide him. Precedent is of little use ; rules and precepts of less. All that the judge can say is that the good, in this place, is felt to be good, and the bad to be bad : aptness is all. So soon as we lay down a law, some violation appears, which yet we own to be right : it satisfies like some "palmary" emendation of a corrupt passage in the classics—it is the exact thing, and no more can be said. The *mot juste* has been borrowed, but it suits the Israelite as it suited the Egyptian. Those phrases which answer the great idea, which *precisely* correspond with the design, and fall into their place as if they had been meant to fill it from the first, these are the thefts which, in dividing the ownership between two possessors, do not take away from either, but actually enrich both.